BREATHING FIRE 2

Breathing Fire 2

CANADA'S NEW POETS

EDITED BY

Lorna Crozier & Patrick Lane

NIGHTWOOD EDITIONS

ROBERTS CREEK, BC

2004

Nightwood Editions
R.R. #22, 3692 Beach Ave.
Roberts Creek, BC
Canada VON 2W2

Edited for the house by Silas White
Cover design by Tim Franz

Typesetting by Carleton Wilson

We gratefully acknowledge the support of the Canada Council for the Arts and the British Columbia Arts Council for our publishing program.

LIBRARY AND ARCHIVES CANADA CATALOGUING IN PUBLICATION

Breathing fire 2 : Canada's new poets / edited by Lorna Crozier and Patrick Lane.

ISBN 0-88971-195-X

1. Canadian poetry (English) – 21st century. I. Crozier, Lorna, 1948- II. Lane, Patrick, 1939- III. Title: Breathing fire two.

PS8293.1.B74 2004   C811'.608   C2004-904473-7

PRINTED & BOUND IN CANADA

Contents

As in puberty I dreamed my lifelong protector, who showed me
How to navigate impossible rivers, who made me as the world's
        first person, breathing
Fire and poetry
. . . .

And I am become the powerful dreamer who dreams his way through
To reality, to enter and ignite the stone, to illumine
        from within
Its perfect paradox, its name.

—from "Manitou Poem," *by* Gwendolyn MacEwen

Introduction

Those are all stories;
the pride, the grand poem
of our land, of the earth itself,
will come, welcome, and
sought for, and found,
in a line of running verse

–"The Pride," John Newlove (1938 – 2003)

One of Canada's great poets of the twentieth century, John Newlove, died on December 23, 2003. We want to dedicate this edition of *Breathing Fire* to his memory. When he was the age of many of the writers here, he was at his peak, a model and source of admiration for his peers, his photograph appearing on the cover of Canada's popular newspaper supplement, *The Star Weekly*. Decades later, in an essay that appeared in a 1983 issue of *Grain* magazine (Vol. 11, No. 3), John in his laconic way, gave writers, whatever their age, some good advice: "Poems, in the end, are not essays written in an odd form. Poems are poems. And none of us may use that Eichmann-like excuse, 'If I hadn't done it, someone else would have.' Here it applies in the opposite direction. If you don't do it, who will? We must do what we must. . . . I wander, I wish I knew more, but you must find your own solutions."

We dedicated the first *Breathing Fire* to Al Purdy, friend and mentor. His two editions of *Storm Warning*, in which he introduced the poets of the sixties and seventies to Canada, have been our models.

When we showed Al the galleys of the original *Breathing Fire*, he wrote, "These are excellent poems, much better than the work of my own earlier generation. They are here by an act of magic, ripened and full blown, youthful yet experienced, a gift we have given ourselves." If he were here to read this new group, we know that he'd be equally as generous and effusive.

Thirty-three poets grace these pages with new and startling work. There are sixteen women and seventeen men, an accidental balance we didn't strive for. We refused to pay attention to gender just as we refused to pay attention to geography, race, colour or sexual orientation. All we wanted was to give poets from across Canada an opportunity to present their writing. Our concern was not for the bias of a particular genre, but for the good poem finely wrought. The voices presented in this anthology confirm what we have always believed: that there is room for every kind of poetry regardless of taste, attitude or concern.

The thirty-three poets here were born between 1970 and 1980. They come from Toronto, Vancouver, Calgary, Winnipeg, Halifax, St. John's and Montreal, but also from Bracebridge, Huntsville, Sechelt, Sudbury, LaSalle, Smooth Rock Falls, a small farm in Saskatchewan and a rocky west coast island called Lasqueti. They and the personae in their poems live among their neighbours where most days they look ordinary and well-meaning. Some mornings they wake waterlogged into regret, and some nights they throw roses from their roofs into the snow. College graduates, fishers, teachers in Japan, parents, orphans, filmmakers, civil servants, comic-book creators, short-order cooks, they philosophize, they add up numbers, they fly night-blind into jazz riffs, and always they write poems.

Over three hundred poets submitted work to this anthology. It was what we expected after having edited the first *Breathing Fire* back in 1995. Once again, in the decade between the last anthology and this one, we'd come in contact with so many talented writers of this new generation in our teaching, our travels across the country, and in the publications of small presses like Nightwood, Brick, Coach House, NeWest, Thistledown and Gaspereau that keep poetry alive. Like the last time, we were amazed, perhaps even more so, by the sophistication and talent of this singular age group. These are the inheritors of Purdy, Nowlan, MacEwen, Ondaatje, Newlove, Wallace and Atwood, the inheritors of McKay, Zwicky, Mouré, Brand, Musgrave and Lilburn, but also the inheritors of Babstock, Solie, Bolster, Bowling and Goyette. Though the majority of the contributors to the first edition were relatively unknown at the time of its publication, the writers in this edition have already received astounding recognition. Their biographies list grants, awards, book and magazine publications, editorial positions and other strong signs of growing literary reputations. This generation seems to be savvier than those in the past about how to get by in a world that doesn't reward such an esoteric endeavour.

Like other anthologists, we want to apologize to the ones who did not make it into this book. There was so much good writing submitted by poets in this age group that we could have included fifty instead of thirty-three writers. The last cut we made was painful. No doubt, we've made mistakes and we've overlooked someone. Our only comfort is that other collections continue to be published and the good poets will all eventually emerge. This collection owes much to Silas White, the editor of Nightwood Editions. His dedication and hard work are evident on every page.

Will there be another *Breathing Fire* in 2014? We have no doubt. The tradition begun by Al Purdy and continued by us has, we hope, a life of its own. Whether we do it or someone else doesn't matter. A great land will always create a great poetry and it will be heard if only we dare to listen.

John Newlove in his *Grain* essay says, "There is a song of some kind in every heart. . . . I believe that some of those songs, lyrics, will always escape into the open air to be heard by others." Here are some that have escaped. Read them with your ear as well as your eye, as John suggests to all who turn the pages of a book of poems. Read them with your heart.

Tammy Armstrong

Tammy Armstrong's writing has appeared in literary magazines and anthologies in Canada, the US and the UK. She has a BFA and MFA in Creative Writing from UBC. Her first novel, *Translations: Aistreann* won the David Adams Richards Award (1999). Her first collection of poetry, *Bogman's Music,* won the Alfred G. Bailey Award (2000) and was shortlisted for the Governor General's Award (2002). Her second collection, *Unravel,* was published in 2004. She currently lives in Halifax, NS.

A Proper Burial for Songbirds

1. *Partita*

Boreal winds through Howe Sound
edge the birds away from the island.
This morning belongs to them:
last survivors who deny the solidity
of the earth beneath their flight,
fall and glide like too many laundry tickets
from dresses I've forgotten who removed.

Autumn is house paint, thick with rain.
Soon, they say in the cove, soon the rains will come
in November when the songbirds go,
when the broken-necked, bruised axillae
are washed down past the property lines
buried beneath buck-trodden mulch.

Pincette-mouthed, their songs push out
past early morning, hole-punch the mist
still hanging over Valhalla.
This charm of finches strips the lilac bush of beetles
sits high on the scattering of car parts the neighbour collects.
They are halation,
the sparks and embers from our unattended bonfires
stretched toward the skewer of low tide,
sparks that settle over damp beach stones
glow, breathe quickly as I have beneath your hands
in those plumb mornings before the birds woke,
began their songs again.

II. *Aubade*

The kitten brings a dead goldfinch to my desk,
weasel-bodied magus has no need
for these tokens of praise.
I leave it near the dictionaries and recipe cards,
wait until the sun slips through the pines,
lamella rays through the backyard
through this hutch of a house I call home:
the hinge-stiff door, stained coffee mugs,
the rhubarb stalks, always mealy before picking.
The cats will not forget,
they lose interest, as I do with too much.

This Sunday morning, late summer.
Sunday not for burials but for cricket wheeze,
a lawn chair, chainsaw whine some miles away—
we have lost the cadence between us.
I no longer remember where your significant scars lead,
light cigarettes too slowly this morning
and the room burns with singed tobacco.
It won't wake you.
The birdfeeder was blown down last night—
the squeak and pull on clothesline—a grace note
while songbirds in gypsy brights peck over blighted lawn,
over the gold leaf rings where the rattans stayed all summer,
softening then splintering under the afternoon suns.

A dead finch
pale as the anemic yard trees,
skull feathers nearly the colour of infection—
I slide it outside on old newsprint
watch as it falls unapologetically
on the rusted fronds of last year's wood ferns.

To Beat a Thunder Shower

Thick as the smell of an old uncle
who laughs to avoid hearing you,
whose clothes are always closer to grey than white,
who speaks of a woman named Sally
after you've refilled his glass for a fifth time.
A woman named Sally, the air says now
as clouds pull out until their fibres strain,

we will not last, they say.
We will not last, he says
as a shell of neglect fissures beneath ribs.
Thunder falls like a tumbler in a drunken fist,
hard and fast, hard and fast,
scattering sound beneath ash trees, secondhand couches.

REFLECTION ON WHAT WAS MISSING

No reason to keep up the ruse,
we're all leaving now
the crows have taken over,
they sear through morning—
car oil, hovering
slick above the trees
morning soundtrack—
their presence
smoker's lung black
wheezing through gossip
slipping into trachea
until the air itself is black
feathered with grief,
with laughter
that never ends, never begins.

HOCKEY

Hockey rumbles through Saturday afternoon—
ashtray peaked with Dunhills
microbrew for breakfast.
An acolyte of the great Northern tradition
you chant at swag-bellied athletes who shoot
one-timers across the screen while I
read a borrowed book, sip warm beer.

Canucks, Red Wings, Islanders—
all words I've now learned to use differently.
I've mistaken a Shark for a Star
really believed there were two Odjicks.
A practice is cracked-ice pronunciations
Czech rolling out of announcers' throats
like chili dog, Molson, hat trick.

I pretend to comprehend icing
try not to think of children's birthday parties
which always end in tears and bad photography.
Offside, high sticking, slashing—
all parts of relationships gone bad, I thought.

When the TV shorts: mock plays,
preprogrammed radio
the backup: you
in military sweater and boxers
sliding over the floor
stepping over books, plates, cats
toward some net
somewhere near the refrigerator.

This season goes on forever
the rains will eventually thin
bring back Vancouver's panhandlers, tulips
yet we'll still be here each Saturday
watching blurry figures skate
through the static of an old RCA.

I am Canadian without heart, I suppose.
My ignorance of national sports so obvious
on buses, in bars, these terms:
we are always at the blue line
at the unpronounceable words between us.

Sheri Benning

Heather Benning

Sheri Benning grew up on a small farm in central Saskatchewan. After receiving an Honours Degree in English from the University of Saskatchewan, she co-founded the Saskatchewan-based chapbook publisher, JackPine Press, and later completed an MA in creative writing at the University of New Brunswick. Her first book of poetry, *Earth After Rain* (Thistledown, 2001) was the recipient of two Saskatchewan Book Awards. In 2004 she won the Saskatchewan Lieutenant-Governor's Award for achievement in the arts and the Alfred G. Bailey Award for her second manuscript of poetry, *thin moon psalm*.

BEARLETTER/2

Bear,

I have never given birth,
my womb a spring plum,
clenched fist,
sleeping sepaled flower.

But Bear, you teach me birth, your name a verb,
hulked muscles river-roll over your bones
as you hunker. Your holler guttural as
earth tears beneath your paws.

Birthing room, a cave, ice-white walls.
Hibernation over, you hunger-howl.
You are beside   inside
coming out—
      You burrow through a leaf shadow,
emerge from a labium shrouded by
shavegrass, ragweed, passionflower.
Your fur is slick with symbiotic
swamp you left behind. Hunger-howl—
nipples sun-hard chokecherries.

Everywhere your fetid musk:
cracked skin   marsh root
blood   moss   scat.

RUSSIAN THISTLE
for my father

I want to tell you about
the Russian thistle in the ditch
with flax and clover, dusk's
first stars. How standing
in low sky, a hungry mouth,
sweat buds on my body. Barley
bows beneath shadow, wren-
feathers my legs.

I want to tell you how
the sun behind clouds
is an opal, everything
dusted with motes of
flexing light,

and clouds clenched
with silt-veins are wrinkles
in your brow or crescent
clay-moons beneath your nails
from a lifetime seeding
and harvesting.

I want to tell you
about the Russian thistle
in the electric light
of the opal sun, moon
still a frozen whisper.
How a crow-breath
before rain punches
earth releasing
the green of sage
and sap,

the barbs around
its heart remind
me of a beauty
so sharp that
when it enters,
it never leaves.

THE BREATH OF LOOKING

I)

The great horned owl underfeather you found
suspended on brome teaches you about the near
imperceptibility of grief. About thinness.
How light, hardly snared by down,
filters through and changes just-so
and so grief wears you, makes
you its slight shadow.

II)

The great horned owl underfeather teaches you
about the eyes of someone you long for. How if they could
stroke you, they would be as graceful as the almost
weightless. How if you could look at the sky
through them, you would feel smaller,
but not less.

III)

The great horned owl teaches you that the knack for
flight has something to do with silence. Its wings polish
planes of air; distance shimmers in their wake. In the after-
weep hiccoughing hearts of poplar leaves, how
to feel the silk breath
of looking.

Womb

: petal-curled in the garden of my mother,
beneath the moth-drone of her lungs, in her

wish and blood; before my voice became
descent; before language, the sound of distance

between what is divided ~

every word I say, traced back to first exile;
every word, rooted in parting; every word

is echo for the web of her
moth-drone, wish, and blood.

Amy Bespflug

Joe Denham

Amy Bespflug was born in the Columbia Valley, BC. She has lived and travelled throughout Mexico, attended university in Victoria, BC, and currently lives on Lasqueti Island where she is at work on her first collection of poems and a novel.

WINTER

She walks through columns and columns of oak trees
wearing only a red Mexican skirt. Vultures and crows,
black rabbits and an old mare follow her. She walks and walks
but doesn't get anywhere, the oak grove stays the same,
no leaves on the branches, no clouds today. All of this happens
very slowly, and although the girl doesn't know where she's going,
much later and far away she will dip her brush into red
and paint October, the canvas propped on a wooden chair
beside the kitchen stove, a pot of water boiling,
her mug with tea leaves waiting. If she could see the girl
walking through the world inside her, the old painter might say,
Her bones in the sun were horsehair, strung
like strands of water from the fence she would become.

In her bathroom there is a deep porcelain tub
with gold feet and a tall window full of clouds and wind.
The roof leaks rain and a candle burns because she knows
dusk is coming. Washing her hair, the old painter bends into the bath
and pours water onto the back of her neck with a mason jar.
Through the window there are rooftops and birds then the Olympic
      Mountains
collecting snow and beyond that there is only what she remembers—
the streets still warm in September, her bare feet, an afternoon coal train
she hopped once to Golden, her horse's bones like a river she rode
bareback behind Indian Head, a black bear eating apples in the backyard,
her body in the hospital with red gauze around the wrists.
I will paint the way my blood painted water, she says.
And her hair like fan coral spreads in the currents.

WANTING THE DESERT

Small clusters of rain on the window and again she thinks
pregnancy, disease, crow feathers scattered around the box heater,
the burnt kitchen linoleum, the dirty stove. How she returned to the
      whales
calling in the dark, to the cold sand that led her there, to sunlight
through the east window undressing the naked things in this room:
his sock curled by the bucket of empty soil, rosemary
bundled by a twist-tie and drying, this complication
of spine and linoleum, her hands wanting only to be there.

Hard to Hold Rain, Harder to Hold Light

As many cricket sounds as stars in the trees behind my house.
I'm writing to tell you many things, but the sky isn't bright enough
to sun this paper. Today the rain is silent. It won't sound
on the things that meet the end of its falling: leaves, tinfoil and cereal
    boxes
in the garbage pile, the garden that isn't growing anything.
But all of this is small. I hear you've stopped talking
and you're living in a room in a ward in the city
without windows, only walls. Yesterday I photographed
broken things for you, for your silence
in the room: the inside of a plum I tore open and the summer
I heard leaving from there, the four untuned strings of my violin
still quiet when sun through the window sounded
across them, my feet separating water from water in the bathtub.
Please remember August ten years ago.
Remember biting a wasp stinger out of my palm
when I collected a wagon full of pop cans we got rich off.
Remember the scars on my knee because you slammed the brakes of
    your bike
too fast in front of me after the neighbour's goat chewed open its gate.
My mother picking out the gravel with tweezers
while you sat on the toilet beside the tub I filled red.
Years later, the night we drove across the Columbia
on a logging road, headlights tunnelling the forest.
The car turned off, the mosquitoes, the warm hood, the ticking
    radiator.
It's hard to hold rain, you said. *Harder to hold light.*
And I'm writing to ask if you will tell me this again.

YESTERDAY

I will fall in love with him because
he raped me, horse hooves clawing
at the dust surface of his eyes, vultures

circling inside my rib cage, neck bent,
head against the stove, all the windows open and
sun on the kitchen floor with me, my hair falling off

like black feathers I will sweep up later trying
to know where I went before I decided
it is easier to tell myself this is love and

remember it was snowing.

WATER

Let me tell you how I came to you, my skin
wet in the dark and steam, bare skin sliding
on the toilet seat, me naked or half-wrapped in a towel,
I can't remember, this memory always changing.
Did I tell you I watched your penis grow underwater,
a kelp stem, two floating bulbs, pumice. Pressed
all the places I have been barefoot
into your chest, stomach. Touched the tip and with my toes
slid back the skin there. How your mother did this to clean you.
And your sister in the maid's quarters. You hate
that you had maids. How the maids did this
and no one ever saw. Your reflection on the taps is cut rose petals

or two eyes with you broken on them. I am too young
to tell you about love. You are eating popcorn in the bathtub
and it smells wrong in the steam. Am I to entertain you here?
A drive-in, the old light shows. Let me tell you I will die by drowning.
It will be beautiful and I will dive after a fin whale too deep
to reach the surface without inhaling water. The water
will be sheets of silver tongues, a thin stretched mercury
surface farther than the bottom so I will have to keep going
deeper into this blue of months at sea. That was my foot
under your penis. Open your eyes. You must see me
here in this bathroom with the light bulb crackling out.

December

I will fall away like dandelions,
bones of sun picked and tied
at the stems with a shoelace, buried
in the wind of an Appaloosa's field
where there are aspen trees
and a tractor without wheels sparrows
have built their nests in. I will remember
last summer I saw the moon
in a puddle and an earthworm swimming
across craters like a seahorse, lavender
drying on the windowsill, the kitchen floor
warm where two cats slept, milk
frozen beside my bed.

Shane Book

Marc Franklin

Shane Book was born in Peru and raised in Canada and Ghana. He earned undergraduate degrees from the Universities of Western Ontario and Victoria and graduate degrees from New York University, where he was a *New York Times* Fellow in Poetry, and the Iowa Writers' Workshop, where he was a Teaching-Writing Fellow and winner of an Academy of American Poets Prize. He has been a policy analyst for the Royal Commission on Aboriginal Peoples, rickshaw puller, grocery clerk and entrepreneur. He is currently a Wallace Stegner Fellow in Creative Writing at Stanford University.

Offering

At the beach, I once saw my father, surrounded by a crowd,
Put his lips over the mouth of a man lying on the sand.

There was something in the way he worked, quickly but precisely,
And without flourish. He could have been nailing shingles,

Or measuring slabs of gyprock for our grey clapboard house
That leaned into the North Vancouver drizzle long before

We got there. As a child, it always seemed to be raining,
So that now, years later, returning to the city, it is somehow

Strange to be sitting on a woman's bed in a small apartment
In a warm square of late-afternoon sun. And perhaps

Because of the warmth on my skin, I do not think of when
We lived in that rundown house on that street where the neighbours

Wrote *Nigger Go Home* in jaunty chalk letters that stretched
To our lane. I do not think of my mother speaking in the kitchen

Late at night of our leaving, my father forever silent,
In what I came to imagine was the thin music of shame.

Why should I? At this moment, a woman is getting ready
To step out of the bathroom wearing nothing but a silk Japanese

Smoking jacket, and when she does, she will stand blinking
In the bright light, then let her robe fall away,

And in that instant her white skin will shine in the afternoon light.
At this moment, I have not yet placed my hands on her neck,

Cradling it, the way my father held the man at the beach, long after
He realized his breath in those dead lungs was helping nothing

And finally, he quit. The man on the beach would never return
To the earth he was born of. And I too have quit, by leaving.

Which is why I cannot tell you, father, of my own encounter
With shame. How brown my hands look on her,

And in their stillness, how useless. This bright offering
I am unable to take, this pale one that lights up the room.

LITOST: A STYLE MANUAL

I remember reading somewhere
Of a Czech word, *litost*,
                    that means too much
To be translated properly—
A wild mixture of sorrow, regret, empathy
                            an inexhaustible longing.
At one time I would have said
It sounded like all the things
                    we might take from this life
Distilled to the smallest crystal of salt
                            on a blade of grass.
Or the worst possible sadness.

I wonder about that now
                    how something can be possible
Yet infinite
And all I can think of are the countless cracks
                            in the pad of a dog's paw
Raised in mid-stride,
                    body rigid with instinct.
Perhaps in this way instinct is a precursor to form
So that it is not darkness
                    but instinct that hems in
The silhouette of a tree
On a ragged patch of grass in Washington Square park
                    in the strange light of late afternoon . . .

*

Sometimes those old days seem so far away,
With their despair and other stories.

One night a friend called
Said he'd just gotten back from an all-night drive
To try to save his marriage.

The previous evening
                           walking by the Budget car rental office
On Douglas Street
                   he'd stopped suddenly in mid-stride,
Wheeled and gone in.
Minutes later he came out driving
What was left on the lot:
                   a bright red cargo van
For the twelve hours north on mountain roads.

It didn't matter that when he showed up at his old door
His wife would be heading off to work
                           a strange look on her face
The question, *What are you doing here?*
Ringing out across the driveway
                   in the clean morning air.

All I could do was smile and point at the van,
                       he told me, voice cracking,
Say, *Look honey, it's red.*

The past is a loan shark. It lends to anyone.
And you can never pay it back.

*

That word *litost* can also mean too little
To be translated correctly—
A thumbprint as singular as the shade of green
On a blade of grass
A meaning as precise as the tools used by carvers
Who make the delicate figurines
I once saw through a window
Of a shop that sold African art:

                       slender, dark wood,
Heads in the shapes of teardrops,
        bodies long to the ground
        without legs.

Holes had been carved through the heads.
An index card labelled them Shadows,
A name which—
Perhaps because I associate shadows
In some vital way with the soul
And imagine the soul living somewhere
Above the shoulders
           —made no sense to me.

In places in the world
            when a loved one dies
They eat the brain
        to stop the soul from returning.
Or is it to keep it close?

*

Another friend had a different solution—
He locked himself in his apartment,
                                    cigarettes, a case of gin.
When finally he opened the door there was nothing left:
Mirror, armchair, bicycle,
                              plates, stereo, potted plant,
Painting of the sacred heart—
All smashed in the alley below his window.
He'd shaved a strip of hair
                              down the middle of his chest
Was sitting on a carpet of glass
                                    talking on the phone.
A hand covered in cigarette burns
Shielded the receiver as he looked up at us.
                                    It was 4 a.m.
Keep it down guys, he said, *I'm talking with mother.*

*

I don't know what to call those wooden figures,
The name for what's left behind
                              after body, soul, after it all.

And I don't want to.

Something about the past
Makes me want to lathe it down to perfection, to nothing,
                              the finest wood dust . . .

Mark Callanan

Andrew McCall

Mark Callanan was born in St. John's, Newfoundland. After completing a Bachelor of Arts in English Literature at Memorial University, he lived and worked in Leeds, England, for nearly two years. His work has appeared in various journals across Canada and in the United Kingdom and was recently anthologized in *The Backyards of Heaven*, a collection of Newfoundland and Irish poetry. *Scarecrow*, his first full-length collection, was released in 2003 by Killick Press. He currently lives in Rocky Harbour, Newfoundland, and is the book reviewer for the St. John's-based newspaper *The Sunday Independent*.

THE MAN WITH THE TWELVE O'CLOCK SHADOW

Doesn't shave much anymore, has cut himself too often
to keep his fingers steady on the blade; wears big hats that
shade out his eyes; is often broken in love, then scattered;
falls down when he walks, so watches carefully before he treads;
drinks a pint of whisky a day for his health and carries
a six-pack of heat on his hip in case of trouble.
And he's always looking for that.

Trains don't run where he comes from
and the horses are all ship-ribbed with hunger.
There's a woman he left behind, of course,
with breasts as big as brass spittoons and
hair the colour of coins on a dead man's eyes.
But he never thinks of her anymore without reaching
for the straight razor, so he doesn't.

The sun, staring down on a scene with him
placed in a tavern, or on his back
in the middle of the red-dirt road, alone
can predict how long it is until he falls again.
No one else here knows his name.
The vultures, thick and liquid in the evening air,
are dreaming of his bones.

DIVINATION

Like Cuvier, reading the entire bird from the feather,
I'm learning to predict disaster in a drop of rain.
The entire predatory body of the storm will come later,
lightning inscribed on the parchment-ragged clouds.
From your kiss I read your leaving, my body
broken by whisky and tears. But all of this came later.
Picture me now, a sort of modern-day Tiresias, stirring my fingers
in every pool I come across. I favour the rain collected
in dishes left outdoors for dogs. I favour dirty water.

Who favours me? The gods, occasionally, when they bless
the entrails of stray cats with visions of the future;

the rain, sometimes, which drowns out all the language in my ear,
that fills my mind with visions of the sea which seethes and
growls and sees nothing and hears nothing and never thinks
of the future. Let the ships and fish take care of themselves.
Let everything struggle to float above the wreckage and the waves.

Yesterday I happened to pass a birdbath and saw your face twinned.
What is the exact significance of the double?
Love appears in visions as a rose, failing that, the carcass of a horse.
Do you remember? You carved your name in my back with a finger.
But for the lightning forked in your eyes, I would have spoken it aloud.
Flower or carrion? (I can't remember.)
I'm not the one in charge of metaphor.

It's no matter. Some day soon I'll find clean water,
sunk at the bottom of a well or falling clear to the foot
of a mountain, spilled as blood through the bone-thick rocks.
For now I'm off to strip each bird down to the feather,
piece my way from here back to the past we had
together. I'll burn it when I find it, as offering, as prayer.

WHEELBARROW

for Allison

Roll on down this muddy road, the handles
guiding me like two prongs of a divining rod,
only on the slope, it's gravity that pulls
and not water. I'm carrying serious-looking junks,
wood for the fire that will burn hotter
than hell, hopefully, or at the very least,
heat the living room through the winter's cold.

I've got a tuneless song on my lips and the whole
morbid weight of December on my mind, but I don't care.
I'm just rolling this wheelbarrow, catching some kind
of a rhythm as the wheel digs in and releases, digs
in and turns up earth, marking its lone tire track
along the path I travel—drawn by something stronger,
more urgent than the presence of buried water.

THE DELICATE TOUCH REQUIRED FOR CHINA
for Nan

My grandmother's hands were crippled,
twisted like roots sunk deep
into earth—

when she was young
two small birds fluttering
about their duties,

tying a shoelace,
bandaging a scraped knee

and, late at night,
taking my mother
by the hand
and leading her home over the dirt road.

I used to bring her tea
and watch her fumble with the cup,

balance it between two hands, wince
at the delicate touch
required for china.
The cracks in the cup
trailed off into her palms.

I remember her sitting on the edge of her bed,
fingers twisted useless around a brush.

I used to sit behind her
and pull comb through hair,
stringing out her history in tangles,
in waves thickly knotted.

Her hair felt like rope
in my small hands.

I remember her lying in a hospital bed,
still as stone,
seeing her dead at the funeral home,
her hands,
two clumps of earth.

In winter, my fingers ache with the cold.
(the frost sinks deep
into the cracks of my skin)

My hands are roots buried under mounds of snow.

Brad Cran

Brad Cran is the publisher of Smoking Lung Press and a contributing editor at *Geist* Magazine. His first book of poetry, *The Good Life*, was published in 2002 by Nightwood Editions. He has been a frequent event host at the Vancouver International Writers Festival and a participant at the Banff Writing Studio. In 2004 he was awarded the inaugural Vancouver Arts Award Commission in Writing and Publishing. He is currently completing his first collection of creative non-fiction, *Cinéma Vérité and the Collected Works of Ronald Reagan: A History of Propaganda in Motion Pictures*. He lives in Vancouver with his partner and their daughter.

PATTERNS OF LEAVES

It's the absence of sadness that makes you want to cry.
No emotion, or brother to hug. When you scream
the sky turns black and without stars but a single
light that shines from the bar atop the hill.
There are girls and treasure for all. So pack
your life into a dream the size of a pearl.
Carry it to a thousand countries. Take an interest
in wildlife. Comb the beach for the perfect shell.

Lie on your back and feel the wind
with your toes. Crack your knuckles like a king.
Your wallet cannot hold another bill. Some leaves
float to the ground as graceful as canoes
turning through a gentle stream. Others fall
and disappear like shooting stars into a crumpled universe.
A pile of leaves. Your amazement at how they fall.
A drunkenness you feel in your chest.
The wind running through your toes
—anything else you care to consider
can be done here.

CITYSCAPE I

Break it even if it is broken.
Trees and satellites. Black birds
and silhouettes of transformers overhead.
Break it. The lawns that once had mole holes
punctuating green scripts.
A dialogue for ourselves. Break it
especially when it is broken. The necessity
to build tall homes. Hard paved roads.
Break it. Blacktop tongue to billboard blues,
broken down on the wrong side of civilization.
Break it till light bleeds tar. Laying rubber
down winter's wet streets. Break it
into night wounds and the poor
dreams of the rich. Libido sliding down
sharp steel. Break it
past broke, the heart's recession

into dark sky. Break it
into laughter. A child's destructive boot.
Break it into place, recast, outcast.
Wounds dug. Wounds sewn. Break
it to last. Earth's malleable bag and blood.

                                City's swimming bone.

ROSEAU, DOMINICA

At the bottom of the gorge, below the waterfall,
you realize your sense of beauty has been callused.
The hummingbird with opal wings nothing more
than a distraction from cynicism. The hike back
through the jungle a testament to green.
The small town and cobblestone streets that turn silver
with rain. In your mind it becomes a question of beauty.
How when you return the cruise ship will be harbour side.
That worst time of day—not rage or anger but an annoyance
brought on by ignorance, yours or theirs, the shit they buy.
How for that four hours you'll be pegged as a tourist.
It'll take you five drinks to become sentimental again
and you'll quit smoking next year. If you could be bothered
you'd stand at the pier and shout them across the ocean
to an oblivion you hope to never know.

Somewhere back home a man is working
the job that you never had. If you think hard enough
he's married your wife, bought your dog and taken your seat
at the local hockey game. Sometimes you just wish
for a definition of home in one word. Years will die hard

but you remember the fine ones,
the places of beauty, words you expect others to know.
How you speak in local dialects and return home,
in some ways wishing you'd never left. Two years since
a Christmas in the cold. Rum tastes sweetest
in the heat and you've borrowed your last few days
on bad credit. Still there is a triumph in every way of life.
Tonight you'll bunk in a hammock,
a few metres from the beach.
Tomorrow you will choose
your sins by the wind
and tide, and a feeling
that you should now be moving on.

TODAY AFTER RAIN

Today after rain
the streets are bare
and smell only of dust.

The service station is broken
and the cars sleep like bodies of beetles
pinned in line by the careful
hand of an entomologist.

The sky opens like a cabinet
and inside there is blue
but then quickly
clouds move and the door
slams shut. A collapse
of black on the ground

and down each street
there is no sound
or movement at all.

Somewhere this is art.

Somewhere a place like this
opens and an eye peers in.

Somewhere this is a collection
worth polishing. A little red mailbox.
The corner grocer. Streets and gutter grates.

Somewhere what matters matters,
the sky opens and the world is unique,
people come out and the neighbourhood
insinuates itself into the present and past.
For a moment it lasts.

For a moment we are common.

S-21, Cambodia

A thin drill at the headrest to open
the flesh from where the neck joins skull.

Steel cots and truck batteries. Rusted
machetes to open women like fruit.

Brick by brick they filled that school

with cubicles of death. Think of chickens
or rabbits packed tight in piss-soaked fur.

Forget thirst. If they took you to a pail of water,
you'd be lucky to drown.

In the clench, without much sound.

To reset back to year zero—
kill the teachers first.

From the grounds today, you can pay
admission and walk through the yard.

Children running in the back field
used now for soccer and volleyball.

Inside, the walls are lined with victims' portraits
small windows that are impossible to open.

Joe Denham

Amy Bespflug

Joe Denham was raised in Sechelt, on the Sunshine Coast of British Columbia. He has worked a variety of jobs ranging from health-food store clerk in Toronto to prawn fisherman in BC's Georgia Strait. His poems have been published in literary journals including *Grain, Event, BC Studies* and the *Literary Review of Canada.* Nightwood Editions published his first collection of poems, *Flux,* in 2003.

NIGHT HAUL

I etch ephemeral sketches in flat, black water,
swirling the pike pole like a sparkler wand,
the steel spear tip igniting fairy-dust krill
as we drift in to haul up our catch.
An industrial gramophone, the hauler
churns a music of creak and moan
over the rumbling whine of diesel
and hydraulics, the echo of our exhaustion.
We sit astride the gunwale, hunched
and awing at the swooping arc of green
the line bends below the surface,
tugging the boat over the set—

till traps stream like marine comets
emerging from the depths in a burst of glow
and morphing back to bare utility
whatever beauty we'd begun to imagine.

BETWEEN STRINGS

Stoop against the portside gunwale
in a thin slat of sun ducked
under the deck awning, listen
to the wake wash off the stern.
Wish for a long run this time—
our limbs are tired, feet and fingers
swollen—long enough to rest,
watch the Sea-to-Sky steam train
whistle along the cliff. Smoke.
It's this lullaby of the boat's
slow roll through wispy chop
that lightens and sustains us:
as the main hums below deck
we watch our measured approach
to the next string, like musicians
anticipating the wand-wave to allegro.

GUTTING

Peel back the squirming tentacles
and slice the beak out like the stem
of a pumpkin. As I flip its head inside-

out, I can't help thinking *sentience*
of a four-year-old child, can escape
from a screwed-down mason jar, emotions
are displayed through shifting
skin colour. The dead, still-groping body
in my hands is dark, its sepia fluid
soaking into my sweater and gloves.
I bring the glinting blade down and
cut the blue-grey guts away, catch
my reflection in the steel-shaft
mirror: guilt-wracked, gut-sick
for two bucks a pound, fish feed,
tako sushi on Robson Street.

DRAGGING

Heave the heavy, many-pronged drag
over the starboard gunwale and watch it
slap grey water, sink. Somewhere
down there's a whole string of gear
clipped of its lifelines to the surface
by a tug captain playing connect the dots
with our bobbing orange scotchman. Fucker.
We wallow in the doldrums of waiting
while our skipper, eyes pinned to the sounder
and plotter, curses his luck and hauls up
something's rusted sunk something, old algae-
slimed groundline, a cluster of drowned
beer cans. That string's worth five grand, but
there's a limit to how long we can hope

for recovery, when each pass keeps
coming up junk, or empty.

MORNING SET

In the morning the languid rhythm
of waves lapping the fibreglass hull
lulls us from dreams of softer beds
to the catacomb dark of the fo'c'sle.
The tired boat tugs its tie-lines,
bow, spring, and stern, then rolls
in waning slumber, groggy in its slip.
The creak of bumper on tire, the wind-
chime ringing of stabey-pole rigging,
even the gulls' off-key mewling
coaxes us back into foggy half-sleep—
till the shrill clang of the alarm clock
and our skipper's coarse, timbral cough
lifts the dream-load from our weighted eyes
and we rise to his footfall and Zippo-flick—
the whine and sputter of the diesel turning over.

BUS STOP

One sits on a tattered blanket
beside his backpack and cardboard sign
which he has tucked away
for the night. It leans against
the stone wall of the bank:

Spare change for
beer, tacos and porn.

I snigger at this, understanding
in my way this young man, close
to my own age, who is not that far
gone yet: still a fullness to his face, some
body to his *Hey man,* in response to my *Hullo.*

The other comes down the sidewalk
as I take a seat on the transit bench,
his bone-thin face protruding
from a black hoody, the acronym
AIDS scrawled in white
across the back of his
torn jacket. He begins
to pace behind the single pane
of plexiglass between us. My ears
on his footsteps, my eyes

focus on the pack of teenage girls
across the street, the goosebumps
on the muscle boy's arms, the dull
racket of anar-kids bashing guitars
and drums under a KFC awning, the three-
minute interval between cruiser car pass
and cruiser car pass, anything to suppress
the thought of what he and I
may or may not,
now or in the future,
share.

Adam Dickinson

Gabrielle Zezulka-Mailloux

Adam Dickinson was born in Bracebridge, Ontario, where he grew up around the Muskoka Lakes. His poems, reviews and essays have appeared in a number of Canadian literary journals. In 1999 he won the Alfred G. Bailey Prize from the Writers' Federation of New Brunswick. His first book of poetry, *Cartography and Walking*, was published by Brick Books in 2002 and was shortlisted for an Alberta Book Award. He completed an MA in Creative Writing at the University of New Brunswick before moving to Edmonton to finish a PhD in English at the University of Alberta.

PHILOSOPHY IS GOING UPHILL

Feet planted, one after the other,
climbing is syllogism,
the world being built beneath each step,
truth tables locked in the knees.
Someone climbs with you and you are both breathless,
as though each chest were a grasp,
as though holding hands meant
thinking the same thing.

Downhill is memory—slack rope,
spilled drink.
Most of the body is water,
knees can't be the only answer.
They are red herrings swimming,
fallacies of the undistributed middle:
all stars are fires, but not all fires are stars,
all weight is gravity, but the knee
descends creek beds without proof.

You remember, coming down, your life.
All the log cabins of thinking
lean dangerously,
suddenly much farther from town.
Downhill remembers mornings burnt with dark,
the river falling over itself like terrible news,
abandoning the higher ground,
the loose-footed stones.

CONTRIBUTIONS TO GEOMETRY: THE SNAKE

Not simply the garden, the machinations
of splitting such right-angled rules.
Its body is line, but not railroad, or light,
not telephone wire or bridge.
It moves as wilful smoke, leaving the ash of a life
angular as wood, curling up, each curve
a science of forgiveness.
It thinks: forget those crosses and boxes
in the crystals of freezing, in the hardening of death.
To move through the world is to bend, is to give.

Before straightened rivers, there are oxbows.
Before the grid roads of quitting your job, moving to the city,
and trying to find her, there are
the intestinal ribbons of your brain,
the twisted chromatin of sex, the lives
whose scrawled arcs unwind before you
like the coiled spring of a clock.

GLAD ANIMAL MOVEMENTS

The amber of handling pine,
its knotholes of glued air,
its pitch that reminds your palms,
that after dust, and after soil, and long
after the salt of the oceans,
it is stone you will become.

Ice lasts all summer in the saw shed.
Under the pine-dust it smokes as the men smoke,
their cigarettes spotted with pitch.
Among the dismantled softwoods,
this cranial bone, this veined quartz.

Pine is the renunciation of caress,
it is the furious immodesty of a desire
whose blood is the resin in grasp.
Let the last things we touch,
be so ruthless,
so bold.

WHEN WE BECOME DESIRABLE

There is a genus of spruce so enamoured with the sky
it is painful to look at its blue needles—
like watching someone give themselves
so wholly to a doomed love
that you know you can do little,
except be there when the crepuscular heart fails.
Its limbs are the blue under your nails, in your lips
when the cold has opened its umbrella inside you.
In winter, the shadows in its crown
are footprints through a playground in deep snow
collecting the bruised light of retreating children;
it takes some time to recover yourself
after seeing this in the late afternoon.
It is not the kind of tree you can climb,
but often its lower branches hang down
like the sloped walls of a tent you can enter
and be, for a moment, among the pitch and splinters
of wanting, with all the colour of your blue-veined blood,
what will not receive you.

BELIEVING THE FIRST WORDS YOU HEAR

When the axe jams in the log
it is memory
reaching to pull you in.
Cherry is the easiest wood to split;
its grains are straight
paved roads.

Maple makes me think of you;
it grows branches as though
committing to entirely new trees.
I think of the axe handle
alive in my hands,
I think of the leaves.

FORT SMITH FIRE BRIGADE

The ravens are as large and as loud as babies.
They are public tantrums
for food that has dropped in the dirt.
In the town parks, on the hydrants,
they are wood leftover
from a catastrophic fire, a black that gulps
daylight and holds it like a rain barrel,
a locked and scorched water.
They are ambassadors from the other side
of what-has-burned, laughter
that reverberates at the end of language,
rises up, its feathers of thinking smoke.
They treat the things we build
as furniture; the gas pumps,
the stop signs are slouching galleries,
are the relaxed mess of a building
they know they can leave.
A raven is the child that leaps into your throat
when branches have fallen in the street.
It is the part of you that grows younger
when first you realize at night
how well the dark takes up residence
among the open, leafless stars.

Triny Finlay

Drew Kennickell

Triny Finlay was born in Melbourne, Australia and grew up in Toronto. She has an Honours BA from Mount Allison University and an MA in English and Creative Writing from the University of New Brunswick. Her poetry has been published in *Grain, Other Voices, Pottersfield Portfolio, The Fiddlehead, The Antigonish Review* and *Modomnoc.* She is currently working on a PhD in English at the University of Toronto, where she is founding editor of the literary magazine *Echolocation.* Her first poetry collection, *Splitting Off,* was published in 2004.

SELF-PORTRAIT AS MY OWN BRAIN TUMOUR

This, love, is an imagined world.
Things go up and down, in and out
like grubs in the butterfly garden,
like death-ready shadflies, mouths sealed against the future.

Let's talk about the brain, how
it's been murkier than salt marsh water, how
it slips in its own cranial puddles,
will implode without warning.

It's a snake in the grass.
A black pearl.
You can't see it but it knows you are watching.
You can't see it but it hides anyway.

Let's talk about vision, the image you might
have if we'd been in the same dream:
    a sagging barn before it falls,
    a slab of Fundy ice before it shifts,
    a muskrat's tail before it slides into the reeds.

    Carve me. Pry me out.

What good is a kept secret, where does it go
when the pain ends?

SELF-PORTRAIT AS EKPHRASTIC TENSION

Let's call it what it is: desire,
or hope, or chaos. Something

sublime—a gilded frieze you touched
in Brussels, for love, in the public square;

a vase you carried on your back through
Asia because, though it cracked

along the way, you thought it was sacred.
What you should know about hope

is that it can't be pinned down. Either
you feel it or you don't and don't

mistake it for desperation. The old
stone will shift because of your

fingers; sugar peas snap.
The morning light in your living

room will catch every gap
in the vase if you glue it back together.

Snails

We can't snap out of this culinary
exchange for love: tonight he wrenches
snail bodies from their flawless encasements
and talks about baking them in pastry.
He hasn't done it yet, hasn't tried
to uncoil me, hasn't sniffed or probed
my sleep-filled temples for the mark
of a crow's talon, for the sinking of skin
and the unequivocal trappings
of weakness. There would be no foot to stand
on, my bones are scissor-sharp kitchen
tools, ready to separate meat from shell,
cake from springform pan. As if a sudden
slit in the right spot will leave us exiled.

Vinegar

Water or dry shiraz, and nothing else;
I'll pour a glass of each. You are a storm
leak through plaster, tuberculosis
before it is diagnosed. The first
time you drip like an intravenous
solution and I flinch at the needle prick.
Other nights you bead like mercury into
its own tarn and I can't watch you.
I will keep you in vials, save spittle
cells for gauging heat and health and
dips in pressure. The wine won't last.
There will be stains. The mole on my neck
will deepen, emerge as the black moth
you wait for. Soon my lungs will burn.

Boy

He licks the divot of my upper lip.
I sleep until noon, nesting. He says
the deuce is in him, in water,
in cries from the baby upstairs.
Lie with me. Lie with me again.
He shifts at dusk, supplicates and feeds
me secrets whisked into omelette froth.
He will waltz with two men on his
shoulders. He will skin me a peach.
And if he finds me wanting, sleeping? *Heal
water, and from it there shall be no more*

death or barrenness. The house is ready;
I slake the thirst for what I might lose
in order for this wakening to feel smooth.

PINK SNEAKERS

In a tin-roofed town the sidewalks bisect poop-strewn lawns. Watch your step. Mail carriers have known this for years, wear rubber soles, follow mathematical routes. Don't always deliver. If you wear pink sneakers in this town, be warned: kids on skateboards will smile, bank tellers will swoop like benevolent night herons. Walk quickly when you walk at all, avoid standing in lines, choose indoor dining over open patios. If the sneakers are new, and made of suede or canvas, never wear them in the rain. The dye will bleed like beets into your feet, leaving you stained in cotton-candy splendour. If the sneakers are old, wear them everywhere. People you pass will believe in things they hadn't before thought possible, convinced by the value of snug, jarring footwear. But don't fool yourself into thinking it proceeds from here. Eschew pink jeans, pink tank tops, pink cashmere sweaters. The force is sudden, and limited to shoes.

Adam Getty

Peter Sobchak

Adam Getty was born in Toronto and currently lives in Hamilton, Ontario. His poetry has been published in journals in both the US and Canada, as well as in the chapbook, *A Gentle Shaking* (Junction Books, 2001). His first book of poetry, *Reconciliation* (Nightwood, 2003) was shortlisted for the Trillium Book Award for Poetry and won the 2004 Gerald Lampert Award.

GAINFUL EMPLOYMENT

You stand here, a man, useless:
waiting for work
in Paul's gang, or Danny's,
someone else's. In this dark room
let the moments lengthen
and thicken, let others leave the line,
helmets on heads, not in hands.
Remember a time, a year ago,
twist of fear
your name wouldn't be called,
no food for the kids.
Now, calm: nothing to be done.

And then, somehow,
picked,
stand on a dock and wait:
you've taken the bridle
and the load is being lowered
to your back. Grab the steel:
Push, push damn you,
are you a woman?
Spin it round, make it square.
Unhook it, moron, get out of the way!
Wait for the next load.
Look at the lake: faded from the cool blue
by which you started, heavier now,
slow-moving. Forgetting
you held your helmet
in your hand, glancing
at your wrist, when
will this be over?

Drinking a beer at the Picton,
you hear stories:
struck in the head
with a hook, my eye fell out—
doctor laughed and popped it back in.
Guy used to work here,
load fell on 'im—a wife, kids;
they're poor as shit.
You gotta work. Arms, legs missing,
hooks for hands. And now
you feel ashamed,

looking at your hands,
standing on your feet.
Glad for the days
your name isn't called.

from SONNETS FOR RED HILL CREEK

> *The land seems throttled*
> *by the disintegration, but I resist*
> *the temptation to spurn*
> *the frailty of its voice, which, even still, speaks.*
>
> –"Junction Sonnets, III. ii.," Carleton Wilson

I

A hill I used to know: rising gently
though torn by tired machines, patient
with old age, the only face of the world
I see. It still carries the old oak
on its shoulders, sagging a bit beneath
the weight. The skin of the hill, loose,
crumbling, shrinks from wooden bones,
pale dust sliding over itself. There

is nothing human here but the usual
grinding beneath the wheel: the hill
a dead thing, the land throttled—
an inverted mortar for beating down
the limbs of trees, the sea of grass
and all that swim in it.

II

The tree leans as though cradled in another's arms:
this is how I read the scene. Silver-white
flecked with black, branches clasped to its sister-
tree, thin and afraid. Why one that rises,
one that falls? The roots of the fallen birch
ripping through earth, pulling into light
what should remain dark: long, silent bones,
bones not yet dust, bones unsure of their use—

whether to clutch the withered bark, clasp tree
to earth, or let themselves fracture wholly
and completely, become ground to hold other,
more stable roots firm. This thin string of words,
phloem spun around itself in fear, felled
by disintegration I still find strength to resist.

IV

What's left: white hill of chipped flint rising
to level bed for wood, iron. Sloping sides—
step-pyramid
                    or burial mound, eye-
beams gleam on flat ties where pile of stone
narrows to sky.
                    Strength keeps you here, legs
steel trunks to root the swinging hammer,
chiselled spikes driven through dead pine.
                                        Riven
field of trees and creeks never enough:

iron trains rattle over the finished ridge
while new pillars rise, grey, to shadow
the wet road, cement poured to
                                        fragment
the tightening grid, then forsaken: chisel
and hammer
                    sink while tired machines idle nearby,
their frail voices, even stilled, still speaking.

STEELTOWN

I dreamed you had spread out
and taken the city, that it was all a vast
network of steel and concrete
that formed the hydraulic system
of some industrial hell. The giant spoons
that carried molten steel from furnace
to production line were pulleyed
over our heads on hydro wires as we sat
in our backyards at barbecues or strolled
to the cars you had made. We were implicated,
so we kept silent when the spoons tipped:
the grey pouring down to splatter
and run along our streets, while we danced to avoid
the silver flash that flows in every direction
at once. And the memo they read
when I was first hired to work in the No. 2 Hot Mill—
it was posted to telephone poles like a concert
announcement, flashed in neon on billboards.
No mean worker taken this time: the foreman
stepping into a grimy machine mistaken for steel,
crushed to an eighth of an inch.

warren heiti

SD Chrostowska

warren heiti was born in Sudbury, Ontario, and has returned there over the summers to work in theatre. He is presently studying Philosophy at the University of Toronto.

from *the metamorphosis of agriope*

* (ABALONE)

november
lesbos, british columbia

a,

this stone is for holding down this note, this stone is for giving back to the side of the road where i found it, where i stood in the fluorescent light of a telephone booth on an ocean road and stared at this stone while on the line you read a song about turquoise. i wanted this note to be quiet, quiet as turquoise, fluorescence, surf, quiet as the bracelet you left on my pillow, the cracked abalone bracelet that you removed from the music of many bracelets at your wrist.

but as you said: i am not quiet. i have slept for seven months—i am no less sharp for having done so. anger is a galaxy, black milk and flint stars. your silence wounds me as light wounds the blind earth; i try to turn away from it but it is everywhere.

the light from those days was grass light, light of the fragile june grasses that grew on beacon hill. we sat against our fallen bicycles and you told me about your childhood and the day thinned into a thousand thousand stalks of light. it was grass light, reed light, light of whisky-soaked harmonica reed, aster and acorn and abalone light. every day was lit with that light.

i met you under an oak tree, you were biting blackberry thorns from your thumbs. you had a violin with abalone tuning keys, you had that stolen harmonica in a minor key, and while you played piano, the silver bracelets shivered along your bare forearms. you showed me where the blackberries were, and we sat in your car, rain on the windscreen, eating handfuls of blackberries and drinking whisky from your flask. i followed you to the bent tree in the bay, we did not speak and the beach was a stretch of darkness and pale shells, a chart of stars, and wind in the rigging in the distance.

silence is an ear-shaped shell, sea-ear, ormer, mother-of-pearl.

the night of the leonid meteor storm at maltby lake, i lost the mossy mopalia shell, the one the seagull gave me and i kept in my pocket, it was the colour of rusted copper, a carapace of rain. you sat across from me at the bonfire. the hyades came unfixed. a turquoise star tore the sky in half.

the taste of harmonica, cobwebs and blackberries. the evening tuned with abalone. you were already married to the rain.

the last time i saw you, you were a silhouette in your ochre chair by the window, your boots up and braced against the frame. you ashed your cigarette into the window-box and sang, and when it was time for me to go, you walked with me to the ocean. it was so still, not even the murmur of surf, only the long, pearl-grey twilight of water.

this stone is for giving back to the side of the road. i will fold this note and place it on the threshold of your room and place this stone upon it and i will leave as quietly as i can.

no, sorrow is not a roadside stone. sorrow is an ear-shaped shell. a silent violin. an abalone bracelet.

o

* (GEORGICS, BOOK IV)

the bees were dying and it would not rain
and aristaios had read a book bound
in snake leather that said one could get
a hive of bees from the guts of a bull.
aristaios brought the only bull
to the bay where she once brought him
and he cut the bull's throat and went
and squatted by the water and smoked
and waited until he heard the sun's drone.
and aristaios knew that nine dawns
had passed, and he turned to the bull's corpse
and slit his stomach and dragged out his guts,
and the guts were honeycombed and humming.
aristaios knew that the sounds inside
were yellow and black, the rasp of sick leaves,
and now he had a handful of august
and a dead bull, but it would not rain, still,
and still the woman was dead. and the bull,
his lips and nostrils black with nine dawns
of rot, began to yell. aristaios
looked from the hive in his hands to the bull
and the black rapids charging from his mouth
towards the sea. it was too late. by night
the sea would be wracked with gangrene.
aristaios felt the hive fall silent
in his hands and knew that it would
not rain. and he sat down in the sand
and cut open the hive and took each bee
into his mouth.

* (SONNET I.III)

she goes to the oracle, she goes inside the temple of stone where everything has stopped, except the ants panicking across the oracle's face, the face pale and hard from the waters of the hebros, the mouth open, the lips cracked. she stands before the oracle and sings a prayer, and as she sings she watches his closed eyes, his open mouth. she sings a prayer, she asks for water and the oracle does not answer. she sees where the blood has stopped in his throat. she sees where the wind has died into his lips and mouth, where wind has become stone, where stone holds the breath of water and wind is a song that no wind is singing, and she stops her prayer. the ants go across the oracle's lips, they go inside his mouth, they come out of his mouth. she swallows and watches the ants and she knows they mean nothing. they go across his lips, they go inside his mouth, they come out of his mouth. she knows he would not ask for tears, she knows he does not need them, she knows the ants mean nothing and knows her tears mean nothing here, and she weeps, the salt in her throat, and she cannot stop, and she cannot get the song out of her body. the ants go across the oracle's lips, they go inside his mouth. she touches the oracle's lips with her lips and she goes out of the temple.

* (THE DEEP SONG OF PERSEPHONE)

she strokes two notes from the tamboura, a cold pulse under the roads of the song, moulted knives in every alley and verse, the notes erode her voice, her voice darkens and hardens her shadow, hollows out her throat and mouth, hollows out the fossils of wind in her throat, her dance of sand shaped by wind, sand and stone tanned by the shadows of raptors, the shadows of hawks, the ululating dunes of her shoulders and throat, the waterless ravines of her arms, the smooth coulees of her calves, every place her body pivots, her hip and wrist, shaped by wind, thin filaments of basaltic glass, her hair woven with the knives of crows, crows' knives caress her obsidian breast, whet themselves on her jawbone, her cheeks, the flesh-red feldspar of her lips, her lips tensed against her voice, sap of pearwood and sycamore, sap of seven garnets, seven pomegranate seeds, she strokes two notes from the tamboura and the notes erode her voice, erode the root and soul of stone, the voracious root, the volcanic soul, the lava rises in the throat of night, the lava dissolves the fossils of wind and dissolves the body of the one who listens, but what has no voice cannot call lapilli from the eyes of night, cannot call salt and water from stone, no no no no no no no stone cannot call water from stone.

Jason Heroux

Jason Heroux was born in LaSalle, Quebec. He graduated from Queen's University with a BA in English Literature, and currently works as a civil servant. His poems have appeared in literary journals in Canada, the US, Belgium, England, Ireland and India. He is the author of two chapbooks: *The Days Are Hardly Here At All* (Microbe Editions, 2003), which was translated into French in Belgium, and *Leaving The Road* (Mercutio Press, 2003). His first full-length collection, *Memoirs of An Alias,* was published by the Mansfield Press in 2004. He lives in Kingston, Ontario.

Fear Diary

Morning, some smoke rises from a chimney
like a clump of grey hair pulled from a drain.
Young nervous men knock on my door and ask
            if I believe in God.

Coffee trembles in its cup as transport
trucks pass the house. I'm afraid of the grass.
The way it twitches in wind like the tails
            of mice caught in traps.

STORY

One summer night a stranger
threw an artificial leg onto my lawn,

made of plastic, leather, steel.
The garbagemen left it there.

Sunday, my neighbour put on
a yard sale. He rang my bell

and swore, "Christ, you got to get
rid of that thing because people

think I'm trying to sell it. I'm
losing business." All our yards

are jammed together—my other
neighbour grows a garden in hers

and throws a tattered trenchcoat
and fedora over the FOR SALE sign

in my yard, to frighten off birds.
I haven't received mail in weeks.

Last night, I carried the leg to
the lake and threw it into the dark

blue sheets of water where it thrashed
as if waking from a terrible dream.

Dark Jars

There is a place
where doctors
remove people's shadows
from their bodies for free.

A friend of mine went there.

I never saw him again.

But he told me about it
last night in a dream.

"The shadows are kept
in jars," he said.

"The jars are so dark.
They all look the same.
And no one knows whose
is whose."

EVENING POSTSCRIPT

The taxi rumbles
    in the empty street
like a straw at the bottom
    of a glass.
A moment later
    everything is quiet:

the dead have called
    us here to make
an important announcement,
    and all
the grass leans
    in one direction like
microphones during
    a press conference.

The stores are closed,
    but the earth is open.
Our shadows pass through
    the grassy turnstiles,

and the spider in her web
    wakes up twitching
like a small dark glove
    when the hand enters.

TODAY I'M MORE ALIVE THAN USUAL

Today I'm more alive than usual.
I am still Jason Heroux but I'm also
the little doorstep everyone walks over,
and the forgotten ladder left leaning

against a wall on Sunday, and a cigarette butt
on the cold sidewalk waiting to be swept up,
because today I'm less dead than I usually am.

Everyone remembers the crime of when
I walked through an old cobweb.
And the little stone I kicked, once.

So you must be Jason Heroux, they say.
Yes, I'm Jason Heroux, but I'm also
the snowflake falling through the air,
and the next one, and the one after that,

but not the fourth one, or the fifth,
no, just the first three, and then that's it.

THE NEWSPAPER

Incurable diseases. Famine. War.
Yet the newspaper seems so delicate.
Rolled up and wrapped in
plastic to protect it from the weather.

UNFURNISHED APARTMENT

All the curtains
are gone: moonlight
drifts across the floor

like a loose band-aid.
The corners of rooms
are angels with walls

for wings wearing halos
made by spiders.
There are empty clothes

hangers hanging in the closet
bobbing gently in place
like ducks sleeping on water.

Ray Hsu

Bonnie Jean Michalski

Ray Hsu was born in Toronto. His writing has appeared in journals in Canada and the US, including *Fence, The Fiddlehead* and *Exile*. His work has also been scored for performance at the University of Toronto. He is completing his PhD in English literature at the University of Wisconsin-Madison. His first poetry collection, *Anthropy*, was published in Fall 2004.

from BENJAMIN: NINE EPILOGUES

At
one moment in 1939, he extracted
an image of sharpshooters all
over Paris in 1830, on day two of an uprising
already running into the sand, aiming their
guns at the clocks on the towers.

the bullets
slamming into the clock face are a form of
dreaming, for sure;

1.

Benjamin crouched beneath the rotting metal.
Here, there was no such thing
as brick. They had forgotten how wooden planks,
slatted together, made boxes,
made brick. A city of wood could burn
to the violence of a fiddle.
But a city that forgot even brick misplaced even
crumbling. Glass too,
he hid under, shivered.
Bombed out, discarded walls around him
blew finite rooms apart.
The entire place is losing its memory
he crouched. *The city.   The world. There is no map*
that can hold a bomb.
A light searing through the air
passed him. Stopped on the twisted ribbons
of metal across. Up,
he followed the long cone to the
Zeppelin, strange and lazy above. Lying there,
haunting the sky.
Through the archways jagged with glass
he watched the huge
static clock face jut into the air. Clocks, like maps,
insisted.
Benjamin watched it become
the slowest thing in the world.

2.

They say he started to forget early. First,
what things were for. Like corkscrews,
or Bibles, or fur coats. Next,
how things were, when someone asks,
"How are you." and there is nothing to answer.
Then, the way things fit together. With these,
wardrobes, keys and compound words. Last,
Names, the appropriate weight of each face.
Misplacing these was easiest. He could hear them, exhausted,
leave.

3.

«Olá, guardador de rebanhos
Aí à beira da Estrada
Que te diz o vento que passa?»   "Hello, shepherd
                At the side of the road
                What does the brief wind tell you?"
    the narrator asks.
        And the shepherd replies,

           «De memórias e de saudades
           E de coisas que nunca foram.»

"Of memories and of saudades
And of things that never were."

In this class, they have been translating these pieces.

    One word has been difficult; it is at the centre of one of their
    less complete excavations.

Sorrows would be one attempt, and has been a consolation prize for the last half-hour, and for many hundreds of years. *Nostalgia*, meanwhile, something doctors invented in the eighteenth century, is a tool like a spade, a word like many from medicine, the only language to continue excavating in Greece and Rome.

One of the students has been here all his life. He had been terrified all his life of saying things.

Years and years later, he will squint. Squint the woman who sang into the smoky blue. This is a Chet Baker song that leaks into life when ironing, when rummaging through pockets for keys, makes him more addicted to cigarettes. Here, in the dark basement of the city, there is something that we forgot while growing up and leaving home. She sang about things we didn't have room to remember until now when, content to be the last in a line, we took to the nearest bench and sat down to watch the people go. He had forgotten about that   how there was a shirt he gave away to someone he might have loved, how he set an appointment to get a poem pinned on his arm   he chickened out but leaned closer to hear this woman this woman this song by chet baker   singing so slow she close to stopped   in this dark basement where he was, this song tell him why he was here and still alive   chet, who played
the blues
in his own way
he was fond of putting heroin in his body
he was also a man
who fell out of a window in amsterdam

The blues.

"What?" they said. They thought for a moment. "What?"

'*Saudades.*'

One said, "But that would be a different kind of word. It'd be a different kind of translation." Another nodded.

"But 'the blues.'"

'Yes,' he said. 'The blues.'

The professor, breathing, waited.

'*Saudades*. Around it is a thick knot of words, and deep within it is another word, written with the care of a slow hand, *blues*. This language never invented a word for it because it never had to. Before.'

They didn't know whether it was true. *Saudades,* one said silently, testing it out. *Saudades.*

4.

Nazi Paris,   where
the People become an endless film. The Revolution fist, on the other
hand, smashes down lazy doors and takes food. A hungry man has
a fist. One for himself and another for the man beside him. A fist
can feed a baby and can build a house. A fist can be safe.

Take this shovel. It is the enemy of the ground. Use it to write a play
where the shovel appears at the beginning and at the end. The
people are important the shovel is important. If a door is locked, use
the shovel. If a man is wrong, use the shovel.

If I should die on the floor, use the shovel to return me somewhere.
Do not use a splendid sentence the splendid sentence is not a shovel.
The splendid shovel is not a shovel. Do not apologize you are not
sorry.

Tomorrow I will be going on the trolley. I will not be taking the
train. The map I did not take with me said nothing about a way to
Spain. Do not follow me I did not take it.

Chris Hutchinson

Born in Montreal, Chris Hutchinson now lives in Vancouver where he writes and works at any number of jobs ranging from English tutor to bar cook. His short fiction, book reviews and poems have appeared in journals across Canada. In 2003 he received the Earle Birney Prize for Poetry, and in 2004 he participated in the Banff Writing Studio. His first collection of poetry is due to be released in Spring 2005 by the Muses' Company. His plans for the future include leaving town forever again and staying alive, somehow.

DISCLOSURE

My friend, always the artist, shows me pictures
of his wife—erotic portraits,
he calls them, claims he wants me
to understand the other side
of his married life. In his eyes
I catch a glint of pride, the roguish
flouting of convention, the smirk
of the saboteur at having infiltrated

the system in order to disrupt it
from within. But there is also a look
of sadness, the underlying grief
of one whose triumphs have come
and gone without praise.
I inspect each photograph
carefully, affect detachment, knowing
that what I hold between us is clearly more
than what either of us will admit. I see his wife
is beautiful, limbs poised as you would expect
of a woman proffering herself to the idea
of undiluted lasciviousness. Only her smile
betrays the mood, her tentative mouth
which holds the beginning
of a question, like the uncertainty
that occurs after desire but before
contentment begins. With the last
picture in my hands, I pause,
just long enough to see
who will be the first to laugh
or blush. But no one does.
How I love my friend! In his sadness
I recognize the silence common
to us both, the quietly entrenched
resignation, a kind of defeat
I'm sick of not talking about. Because now
I'm craving full disclosure, for the moment
to move beyond taboo. I'm waiting
to see if he'll admit bewilderment
at the day he arrived unprepared
for the end of youth's recklessness

and the beginning of an ache
he couldn't explain, admit
the vulnerability all men conceal
behind displays of experience, our need
for affection carried like a secret shame.
Now I'm waiting for someone to let it all
hang out, to confess aloud. For once,
I'd like to hear it said.

THE IDEA OF FOREVER

After last call at three a.m. the sun
on the horizon like a giant lodestar
would guide us over uneven boardwalks and dirt roads
toward the George Black Ferry, across
the mud-fed Yukon River to where our hidden world
of tents lay inside a maze of birch,
where branches knocked and clacked in the wind
like the restless bones of ghosts,
where someone always screamed blue murder back
at the landlocked sled dogs as they cried
and howled at the lingering season
and stunning lack of darkness
inside the night. This was Dawson City
where we'd all come from something
vague: a town, a girl, a life.
Most had simply drifted into the ever-
widening space of summer's north, hoping
to find work, hoping absence,
hard drinking and perpetual light could
wipe the slate clean: it seemed we were all young

enough to trust in the liberty of forgetfulness—
the days blurring without nights, drinking
sour toes with the tourists then
over-proof whisky at the Midnight Sun then
blackouts and waking beside the river
if not delighted, at least surprised
to be alive, soaked and numb.
Had it been a dream, strange-throated ravens
gargling in the trees like drowning men,
or just some lone person
weeping?
In the morning, no one could be sure.
Although I confess, one night
the first star appeared, an unsightly blemish
in the milky sky like a pinprick in the idea
of forever: fall was coming and I was afraid
to travel south, to move alone again,
and further toward the slowly diminishing
light.

AFTER JOHN NEWLOVE

A miserly night sky, November
and Vancouver can promise only rain.

Grasping for a beginning: I've given everything
away, moved again, fled.

What would you do John, make a list of fact? Okay:
at a desk, at an unfamiliar night-blackened window, alone

at last. History gone too—no personal past.
And I've seen the same girl working three nights

in a row on the street out there—her slow, elongated
stride, her pale face amidst the distant city lights—

like an actress before a constellation of eyes.
And this place—

where my little room, it's strange but true,
is painted pink, supposedly soothing

to the unsettled mind, they say—this place,
where a train's whistle claims nostalgia, near-

midnight and a suspicious lack of stars—
this place flickers in the night

like a radiant mind
inside a broken life.

And I wish John Newlove was here.
I'd ask him what the old days were like

sucking the blood from his abscessing tooth,
spitting out poems like divinely wrought curses.

Was it the Age of Aquarius, John?
Or like me, did you crave some other city,

some other time, to ride
off any horizon, anywhere

but through this rain and the grey
eyes of the women you made so unkind?

Is this the same weather you let seep into your words,
your life? Did you hear poems inside the rain, or lies?

Tonight, rain and loneliness have made me strange.
Or perhaps it's this pink room I'm in, like—

like a giant womb! Let's say it is
nineteen seventy-one. Unborn I am dreaming

of escape into the easy giving of a world's love.
Meanwhile, John Newlove wakes at the other end

of a long desire, rolls out of bed, rolls
a cigarette from Bible paper. Lighting the last page

of Genesis or maybe the first
of Revelations, he's suddenly tempted

by a girl outside his window, wants only
to give her words, redeem himself, repent

with savage eloquence, burn
a hole through the mist like a visionary. . . .

Does any of this sound right, John?
I'm sure you lived here once.

Now everyone is gone.

Gillian Jerome

Brad Cran

Gillian Jerome was born in Ottawa and teaches and writes in Vancouver, BC. Her work has been published in *Why I Sing the Blues, Grain, The Colorado Review, Fiddlehead, The Malahat Review* and *Geist.* She is currently completing her first full-length book of poems.

HOMING DEVICES

It started with last month's train wreck.
Onyx sky. A kink in the neck.
I never knew the meaning of unconjugated
until now, the Shitsu dead
and forty ants playing Twister
for a lick of lime. The gods line up. Teeter and huff.
This morning I drank mango juice on the verandah,
wore an ascot, counted goats.
Each horizon is another crawl space
calling for a splendid acid trip, or asphyxiation.
You must believe me, he said, as if
I knew the good books, as if

I had never graced the night's vinyl
with memory of another self.
We carry such false history: the lost child,
the great sorrow, the belt, the buckle,
The Great Escape. And then what?
The belly implodes. Longing. Lips are a soft delta
collecting synonyms for wealth.
Rafters fill with vowels and such
small urgencies: water or dandelions.
I have other excuses for limp eyelids
and a bitter tongue. Men. Women.
They come and go with their garage sales,
their sour perceptions, a certain ugliness
you feel obliged to capture on film.
Love is the illusion your pleasures
will hang together somehow.
It's a crapshoot, this day and night,
these five-and-dime TV dinners,
marmalade streaked across the fence.

PHOSPHORESCENCE

In the cities it wrings through our bodies like zinc. We listen to
ourselves "becoming," arrested by red dresses, while eating sushi à la
carte. The white noise, after all, means something and the shape of
our egos will do. Who to count on but the dark-haired woman who
sells us pizza in front of the Faubourg? Martians live in the
braincombs beneath the city streets and ride the subways reading
Proust, smoking French cigarettes.

Redress, redress the sinner, repent the sins. Inside the buildings at night a certain type of "poetic madness" lights up the cubicles. Every few blocks a billboard and a forgetful city garden. Where a man lies down in front of the oldest pub in town. Beyond the door, a phalanx of husbands in blue housecoats, wives filing their talons at the bar. The verb *to happen* is cloaked second-hand smoke. Some say ants, some say serpents.

We return with this sentence in mind to the banquet of lovelies: "Passion Is Design." To the edge of the city, its green spines, the streets align themselves against a common theory. The beauty here is the bank of twilight and the woman's body junked in the snow.

INTERIOR DRAMA

Can't sleep at night thinking about Paris—
its gargoyles with green eyes & its kings.
Non, je ne suis pas un cheval over & over.
I'm obsessed with the signals left behind
when sleep takes over the body.
Rory's designs on paper, shapes of an intricate mind
of gold cats, half-dead, tangled hands and feet . . .
And the floods—at night I dream of my life
in the rain, holding her while the sky cracks
back & forth—volts of incredible muscle—
taking us in & out of our collective reverie.
First the dark windows, then the jade plant
& her oatmeal breath, all of it descends
upon me in frames: we're all watching *La Malade Imaginaire,*
I'm wearing a short, black number & all the city's dogs

are in heat! She giggles uncontrollably when Argan
finally loses it, remembering that bliss—
an upside-down world unravelled.
Bereft? At the edge of belief in a life
of art & life, I hold her head in my lap
& know that all of our collective paranoias
will manifest, that my espressos in Paris will be black
by the fountain in the quarter she adores.

CONVENTIONS ON A SEDUCTIVE THEME
– after Rembrandt's Bathsheba Reading King David's Letter

How to say no to the visible, to say misunderstood:

    In my little notebook of poems, the sirens, boys in flannel shorts

Within the ice cream of stylish clouds, Paris,

    Will you marry me, will you keep me turning toward mirrors?

Bathsheba skulks the streets wearing a dress of beads

    Free of the master, how he places his hand

All those jug heads wearing loops and spectacles

    Walking through the Louvre & stopping at the female nude

With a mind of her own. Who is she

Outside the sighs of sycophants?

(Her hair—the sack spills and rubies fall—

My mind's eye awash in yellow, ochre, black. . . .)

Jazz boys near the Beaubourg smell her figure in the far-off,

Little iconoclast, her phantom hangs arrested in fog.

The minds of her makers obsessed with the laws of perspective, one body

A burnt door greedy for its ash.

Beauty runs your city with guile, and Bathsheba,

Her shape outside of the mind of a master,

Follows the water to where bodies go,

Among the girth of your sewage, the mind's perfect circuitry,

The clockwork of bordellos that smell of bergamot.

FIRSTBORN

You live in me. We're eating well.

The sky softens into a pulp.

I dream of lampposts,

soft fruit.

When you sleep, you sleep

inside me. White city

covered in ash. Streets

electric with silver,

broken teeth.

Soon little fire

you will live here:

lights and sirens,

sky trains, automatic banks.

Soon you will live here.

Come screeching into the trouble.

Come already haunted.

Anita Lahey

Mark Sutcliffe

Anita Lahey has written about luminescent mushrooms, Canada's worst toxic waste site, the history of rainbows, learning a language and many other subjects for magazines across the country. In 2003 she was shortlisted for the CBC Literary Award for Poetry, won *The Fiddlehead*'s Ralph Gustafson Poetry Prize and placed second in *This Magazine*'s Great Canadian Literary Hunt. She was first honourable mention in the 2000 Bronwen Wallace Poetry Award, and has published work in *Arc, The Malahat Review, Pagitica, Grain* and *The New Quarterly*. Anita grew up in Burlington, Ontario, and studied journalism at Ryerson University in Toronto. She edits *Kitchissippi Times*, a community newspaper in Ottawa, where she lives.

from Cape Breton Relative

Chapter III: In Which You Give In Already to the Urge to Write Home
Tell him, you must, of wind in your shoe, of bats and moths, babies
        tangled
in your hair. Address him as dear. Remind him fog and flight paths
        reappear.

Will he straighten his spine, summon your missives with light
in his eyes? Drink you down with a cold ginger ale. Begin with the
    letter

L. For longing, deeply ladled. Logic, la-la, lust. Latitudes

of pain separated by history, geography. Low-lying strata you never
discuss. Should he know about the three dogs converging on you

at dusk? Your jog interrupted. That night at the concert: beer in hand,
    clammy
ring of hope around your wrist. Silly codes like kite, and hat, and
    smooch. How

you scrambled your names into breakfast dishes, circled the planet
    sampling
expectation. Don't write that the camera has choked on yet another

picture of a clothesline. How many degrees of longitude shouldered
between you now? The bridge that refused to swing you through
    might be a sign

you don't want him to see. Pretend the island is secluded, its intentions
not clear. Read replies like a pilot seeking turbulence. Choppy wind,
    his name.

WOMAN AT CLOTHES LINE
– after Alex Colville, 1957, oil on masonite

Strapped sandals lift the lady
above the lawn. Hung linens adopt her
hippy contours. This is no steamy

Tide commercial. Our star is absorbed
in cooler, wetter realities. She wears
a blue dress, white scarf. Her mouth

twitches wryly into some future. What
rustles toward her through the October
yard? Consider recklessness, how it breeds

in safe places. Was laundry ever just
a chore? Hold a rinsed blouse to your
face. Gaze through its weave at the gauzy

world. Notice how whiteness drinks itself
blue, agitates the fallen red
leaves. Those blankets have been under

your skin; they have things to tell you—
grey, woolly things. She lugs them out
to air their moth-eaten souls. How

gracefully she hoists her basket, all her
disappointments. It's clear from her eyes, the absence
of pins. Nothing here will blow away.

WHY YOUR WHITE TUBE SOCKS ARE HOLEY

You choose which side
covers the heel, always
the same, humming, unrolling

their ribbed necks along your calves
before you run: out the door, down
the porch the walk the road the path that takes you
away from my loving grip. These brief,

sweaty escapes. If only you'd come back
with songs and famished lips. I button

my expectations quietly over your chest. You know
what I like: blues and Billie Holiday, your voice
let loose, wrung socks on the line

squirming to hear. Hold still. Let the music
run through your shredding heels. Listen
for when he doesn't need me. His ballads, his

filling me partly: all that is rundown, trailing
off-key. Thank God you know how to

sing, shut me up, close
my eyes as you touch
your voice to the sky.

THE ELEMENT OF CARRYING ON

Therefore does the wind keep blowing
that holds this great Earth in the air.
For this the birds sing sometimes without purpose.

−"Adulterated," Jack Gilbert

The wind doesn't know what it wants
any more than we do. It grabs what it can
and blasts its way through mortar, barrels
down the chimney. Some days it saunters up
and unhinges the door. Now the wind
is walled in with you and me and the dust and the three
model boats, red and built by a guy named Keeping. It lies
heaving like an old hound on the carpet, giving off
mustiness, sweat. The wind dreams of hunting, kicking
its weary legs. It too can swim. All of us try to remember
where we've been, the things that were so important
to see and do. How many oily foreheads flattened
against the glass, turning to the cluttered room
and then, confused, back out to the bay? We look for
the desperation that once propelled us over mountains.
Five, eighteen, twenty-four hours away, thousands
plunk into blue seats on runways, wait to be flown
into prevailing winds, away from those places
they happen to be. Some days I am among them, or
wish I was. I would give up barely holding
ground against the gale: lodge myself in its yowling
maw, snap off calmly in the din. But I keep coming back
to these boats that aren't boats, to you and our rising
mounds of curled-up air that once commanded
wild dogs and oceans, and shaped the pliable trunks of trees.

INTO THE WOODS

The only geography
we have is the storybooks of our childhood.

–"Eating with the Emperor," Jack Gilbert

Never mind the wide world. In the universe
of grade three you will tire of puddles, plunge
your hands into cubbyholes, fractions, all the dark
rooms you are led to, unwitting. They speak of futures
without cease, as though the answer can be reduced
to that tendency, this task. Accomplishments of love:
children, pets, gardens, dreams. How to sketch & pound
them into shape. This might be possible. But the forest
calls, is always calling. Some of us learn to pretend
otherwise even as, bitten and ivy-bled, we lurch
through labyrinths, shadows. Ice-chunked swamps. Awe
is all we have. There were two kids, that wavering
line of crumbs. The unmistakable river-rush. Follow it
down. Thirst is designed to win, after all. You cannot
name the trees. Their hieroglyphic skins pink the palm, giving
up no clues. Sit. Flatten your back against the mystery
found in the first picture-less book you read, and read
again—the only question the hero fails to undo. Was it
part of the story, or did you insert it yourself? Imagine destiny.
It doesn't matter whose. An endless tree-trunked metropolis
gathers us up by its soiled, elbowing roots while we are tying
a shoe, pushing the carrot across the plate, standing
in rain wondering what has made us
stop, here, on this corner, now.

Amanda Lamarche

Corey Lamarche

Originally from Smooth Rock Falls, Ontario, Amanda Lamarche moved to Gibsons, BC, when she was eleven. She received her BA in English from the University of Victoria before moving to UBC to study for her MFA in Creative Writing. Her work has appeared in *Grain, The Malahat Review, Room of One's Own, The Antigonish Review* and *Prairie Fire.* She is the current poetry editor for *PRISM International.*

FEAR OF BEING ASKED TO DANCE

It's the starting position, the untaught
beginning. Not when the two dancers
step in, eyeing each other, not when
their arms latch lightly, becoming
a fence around their bodies. What you
mean is the *true* starting position. You,
running your finger over the mouth
of your wineglass, a man crossing
the room thinking, *Red hair tumbles*

down her back. You are singularly
aware of the measures between yourself
and every person in the room. You are
convinced that you will never dance
with any man in the indelible way,
his foot following where yours just was
and so forth, on the dark hollow sticks
of a field floor, tangled hands appetent
in your hair, your cotton dress pressed.

FEAR OF DYING TO THE WRONG SONG

There is no such thing as slowing this down.
You are on your way to a day you planned
to spend alone. You now know only that you
are alive in the taxicab, seconds before it pours
itself around a pole. You hear the prayer
of the driver, a woman yelling through the inch
of your opened window and then neither. Just
the song coming softly through the system.
And it is not the kind of song that makes you
hang your head in your hands, give up,
not the gravelled voice of a poisoned smoker
about to outlive you. It is not a Christmas
carol or a hymn that lets go of you. It is
the soundtrack of a hand on your back,
the way your mother hums when she picks
up the telephone. It is the translation
of the story of you dancing with ribbons
tied to your wrists. You are thinking of it

as you clamour to the curb, as you prop
yourself against the collapsed salt box.
You can still hear the strings. Kissed
on the face by a leaf, you cannot bother
to remove it. You know when the song
picks up. You picture the cello being
crushed between the knees, the pianist
pedalling in coal black shoes, the femur
of the flute in the flautist's lap, shining, geared.
There is the taste of that steel on your lips. You
inhale to make any sort of sound. You
almost place your mouth there and breathe.

FEAR OF HOUSES BUILT ON CORNERS

Kerrobert, Saskatchewan. January 12, 1987.
The local paper prints the usual information:
weather conditions, car make, year, speed of entry.
They say the Smythes weren't home. Rocheleau,
the driver, age 25, was passing through. They print
as a joke beneath the photograph, that Rocheleau
needs a ride if one's available. This is the exact
spot they would have written the name of his wife
had he died. Perhaps a smaller photograph of her
lumped against the trunk. But this is not what eats
me, the ill humour. Come into the yard, across
the tape to the burial of shingles. See the fine edge
of the car inside the kitchen. Find the spoon settled
on the hood, the potato box painted as a birdhouse,
shocked in the corner. Nothing said of the oven mitt

in the driver seat, the chair still tucked gentlemanly
beneath the breakfast table. No mention of the snow
moving in on the sugar. Now the tipped cereal bowl.
Now the shelled egg.

Iroquois Falls, Ontario. February 17, 1970.
Night after night my eldest son plucks her stone-
drunk from the couch and carries her to the road.
There, he lowers her against the guardrail,
and himself, so she has something to lean against.
The first few times she broke in, it was nightmarish,
but now it's more a study in sadness from the front
porch, watching the two thin figures in the passing
headlights. I guess after crossing the tracks,
this is the first house she half-sees in her stupor. Maybe
the easiest to break into. Or perhaps it's more, my son's
arms around her, the warm burst of his jacket. And
the smoke of the cigarette he lights up beside her
in the snow. Like a smell that borders on warning, it
excites, it always wakes you.

Tramping Lake, Saskatchewan. August 9, 1998.
A ghost will choose to visit a house built on a corner
before it chooses one in a row. At age 9, Anna
destroyed my sleep without knowing it. Until then
I believed teeth under pillows, cracks in the sidewalk,
blue for boys, that sort of thing. I believed that if you
buried a bee alive in the sand, it would turn to gold.
At the grocery store, Anna named every apple there

by kind proving she knew things, said she was safe
at the lake since ghosts have no need for water, asked
what *I* was going to do. Fifteen years later, I write
a poem where I bite the skin of a red delicious thinking
of her. I tell her the cold spots in her lake are the dead's
last breath and why don't you go swimming? Saying it
aloud, I know it's ridiculous. She is living somewhere
in Quebec and never thinks of me. But let me also say this:
a lady bug moving across her arm enough to startle,
the sound of hands up her banister, awake
to find a pale orchard of loons at her yard's edge.

THE MUSICIAN'S HAIKU

You can make music
of anything, I am sure.
The glass in the wind,

the clay bowl with one
tiny mandarin inside,
waiting to be mouthed.

Even of silence;
the cracked violin curled tight
in the bed, its sound

asleep in the bend
of your elbow. Not knowing
what to move, I trace

your still lips until
a mouth exists. *I'm sorry,*
I say when you wake,

my fingers, the flutes
that were made and then broken.
I'm sorry, as you,

half-remembering
you are not alone in this
room, take up my arms

like bows to your throat
when oh, it is sick to see
my own hands on you.

Chandra Mayor

Karen Paquin

Chandra Mayor is a Winnipeg writer and editor. She has worked with *dark leisure magazine, CV2* and *Prairie Fire.* Her work has appeared in various anthologies including *Exposed: New Writing by Women* (Muses' Company, 2002), *The Cyclops Review '02* (Cyclops Press, 2002) and *Post-Prairie: New Prairie Writing,* and she was recognized for her poetry with the John Hirsch Award for Most Promising Writer. Her first book of poetry, *August Witch* (Cyclops, 2002), was shortlisted for the Carol Shields Winnipeg Book Award, the Mary Scorer Best Book by a Manitoba Publisher Award and won the Eileen McTavish Sykes Award for Best First Book. Her second book, *Cherry* (Conundrum, 2004), is a novel focused on the Winnipeg skinhead scene in the early nineties.

CRISIS HOUSE

1. *The First Time*

The first time was because of my tongue, the way it settled in my mouth like a slug, silent and glistening. The sun shone in squares through the dirty window and I sat in stasis on the green couch for hours, forfeit to gravity, all my molecules engorged and motionless.
   This is what it's like to be a drum full of oil.

I could hear my lover on the phone with my doctor, with my mother, making arrangements.

> *This is what it's like to be a vase of flowers filled with stagnant water.*

They decided that there was no point in going to the hospital; they wouldn't admit me, I wasn't a danger to myself or others, I was merely entropied and mute.

> *This is what it's like to be a tree contemplating the chainsaw.*

My lover packed an overnight bag for me, all the ordinary fixtures of my life suddenly ridiculous: the pink shirt stolen from the dark cave of drawers, balls of socks for severed feet. The world disappeared every time I blinked and I was grateful.

> *This is what it's like to watch fireworks on the insides of your eyelids.*

We got in the car and drove to a little white house in St. Boniface. The back door was locked and we had to ring the bell to be admitted. I was taken to a bedroom, hospital-issue bed, desk, chair. A young woman went through my bag, touched all my clothes, looking for sharps. She took away my medication and my lighter and my glass bottle of sandalwood. I sat on the bed with my knees drawn up and my face in my hands, afraid to speak, forgetting how to nod.

> *This is what it's like to be a nightcrawler, limbless and pink, dug out of the earth.*

My lover held my hand and then she left. The door was closed. My breath was tangled in my ribs and I could only quietly gasp. I slept in all my clothes, sitting up against the wall. I mutely accepted my pills at ten o'clock. There was a black hole in the sky where the moon should have been. No one else came to the door and I was glad and terrified.

> *This is what it's like to wake up in a snowbank with a mouth full of blood, your tongue in someone else's hand. This is what it's like to be bone in the moment before it shatters. This is what it's like to be a rock waiting for the body.*

2. *House*

This is an ordinary house, plastered
with a calm mask of white stucco.
This house is flanked with other white
houses trimmed in blue, green, or red.
This house hides a wooden swing
in the back, a picnic table, a parking
pad, and is hemmed in with an impenetrable
brown fence. On the other side of the fence
is a daycare, and sitting at the back
of this house, smoking a cigarette
and sweating under the merciless sun,
you can hear the children screeching
and you hate them.

This is a mundane house with a large
bay window clouded with curtains like
cataracts. This is a house that never looks
at the park across the street, the sagging
trees, the red and yellow snapdragons.
This is a tidy house with a prim green
lawn, eschewing window boxes,
unadorned. This is a house you drive
past every day and do not see.

This is a house where you are incapable
of looking up.

This is a house that squats stupidly and says
nothing. This is a house with eavestroughs
full of spiders. This is a house that models
banality and flaunts its ordered shingles
to the neighbours.

You are in crisis.

3. *The Second Time*

The second time was because we'd fought about something that I
forget and I cried and cried and I couldn't stop crying even in my
psychiatrist's office I cried and couldn't speak and he told me that if
I didn't speak he'd have to put me in the hospital and I didn't want
to go there so I said No and he called the crisis house instead and
administered the intake questionnaire over the phone while I
dumbly nodded or shook my head

Have you ever tried to hurt yourself
Have you ever committed arson
Have you ever used street drugs
Have you ever committed homicide
Are you suicidal Are you suicidal Are you suicidal

My lover came to pick me up and I was still crying but I put my
hands over my face to hide the bloody scratches on my cheeks and
of course you can't ever really die from shame and she was worried
and I was ashamed and she took time off work and I was ashamed
and she drove me to the crisis house and I lay on the bed with my
silent earphones on to make them think I couldn't hear them and I

cried and my roommate tried to get a nurse because I wouldn't stop crying but I heard the nurse outside the door she said *Crying is what we do here, dear* and I knew I was flattened against a wall and I knew no one would touch me gently and I'd hit them if they tried and I knew I had to keep up my guard and I thought *fuck all of you* and I wailed like a child and I cried and I cried and I cried

as generous and impersonal as rain

4. Veteran Fictions

They leave me with the mirror and the light
bulb in the desk lamp. The click of the closing door
is precise, remonstrative: a snapping finger, a locking
.chamber, precursor to panic. I strip the bed and smother
the light bulb in a blanket before I step on it; I know
that everyone hears everything and they're all listening
through the walls, eavesdropping on the snuffling
of someone else's despair, despite themselves.
I'm determined that I will not be discovered. I unbundle
the blanket and the shattered glass rasps against itself
in a small opaque mosaic. There's a picture, there's a message,
there's a narrative that emerges from this fragmentation and it
whispers *touch me   touch me   touch me*   and trembling
I answer   *yes*. My arms are so cooperative, the veins throwing
themselves against the skin, urging liberation, urging passion,
the long sharp pain, hairline thin, the indrawn breath.

This is the crimson deluge of insensibility, the reclamation of
my body, purging entropy and piecing myself together inside out.
This is what it's like inside a waterfall, the torrent in your ears,
the rolling of your body over rocks and rapids. This is what it's like

to bleed to death, alone. This is what it's like to be released,
to cry and cry in rage and shame, impotent, forgotten.

I lie underneath the blanket, skin itching
against the wool, cowardice licking the tears
from my eyes and the desk lamp bleeding
light, all the shadows unvanquished. This is
only what I wish I'd done, my secret,
sweet and warm, my scarred and veteran fictions.

5. *Benediction*

This is a benediction for your ambulatory
body, a blessing on both the legs that carried
you through the door and up the stairs.
You went forth and shattered and your shards
of self increased a thousand-fold but o
your skin sealed you up and only split
a little at the seams, and you came
back. This house welcomes you like a mouth
and caresses you like swallowing, your swollen
eyes and overnight bag, your toothbrush
and your confiscated matches, consecrated.
Don't hold out your clammy palms in supplication.
Receive gladly that which you are given.
There will be no concessions. This is the hallowing
of fear and shame, the suspension of time, the cataloging
of your failures made flesh, and crying, upstairs
and alone on a cast-off hospital bed, your own futile
invocations of grace spiralling, heavy and hollow,
inside your ears. This is a blanket to cover
yourself, this is a blessing, benediction.

Steve McOrmond

Steve McOrmond was born in the Annapolis Valley of Nova Scotia and grew up on Prince Edward Island. A graduate of the Creative Writing Program at the University of New Brunswick, he has published poems in journals coast to coast, and in *Landmarks: An Anthology of New Atlantic Canadian Poetry of the Land* (Acorn Press, 2001). He has served as an editor with *The Fiddlehead* and *Qwerty*. His first book of poetry, *Lean Days,* was published in 2004 by Wolsak and Wynn. An earlier version of this collection was awarded the Alfred G. Bailey Prize from the Writers' Federation of New Brunswick. He currently lives in Toronto.

FINCH STATION

After a long day, you'd think we'd drag our feet.
But we're all elbows, jostling to catch the next bus home.

The boy and girl embracing near the stairs
aren't in any hurry. Their stillness makes them central.

He is tall and gangly. She, stretching upward
to meet his gaze, one of Modigliani's models,

impossibly long-necked and graceful. The crowd swirls
and eddies around them, the single-mindedness of water.

Neither is saying anything and I want to lie down
in their silence, shelter from the collision of voices,

sizzle of cellular transmission. Just then
the girl's hands scribe the air, flicker like chickadees

and he responds, finger-spelling the words
between them, the body's tones and inflections,

pursed lips, raised eyebrow. Something I remember
reading about Berryman, his secret hope

to be visited by physical disability—Milton's blindness,
Beethoven's loss of hearing. The fortunate affliction

that would rescue him from the machinery of living
day-to-day and bring him to his senses. If they could hear,

would the boy and girl still reach that other place
I yearn for? Looking into her eyes, the boy loses his balance.

They can hardly pay attention to what their hands are saying.

The Burn Barrel

Late October morning,
fields furred with frost,
a film of ice on puddles.
Your job to awaken the beast
from its dreamless sleep, light a match
and watch as it sputters,

                        spits

             sparks.

The plastic bags melt away,
their contents spill hissing
into the barrel—butcher paper
soaked through with blood, milk
cartons, snotty Kleenex, turkey leg
used to make soup, flames licking
what little flesh is left on the bone.

                     You must stay
until everything is smoke and char.
Envelopes with their official correspondence
enclosed, your brother's dirty magazines,
the centrefold shrivelling before your eyes.

You've learned that all things
can be made to disappear. Last season's
Sears catalogue, thicker than the family Bible
and more thumbed over, a book of ash
that shatters when a puff of wind
tries to turn the pages.

APPREHENSION

Walking in the quiet not long after dawn, you find
deer tracks in the soft clay of the old railway bed,
squat down and trace the hoofprints
as though some of the deer's presence
might rub off and leave you
subtly changed. Evidence of another life
going on outside your own. This is the season
of men dressed in bright orange vests, white-tailed bucks
tied to the roofs of cars. And yet the deer
travel the abandoned tracks into the centre of town,
bending under the ghostlight of stars
to nibble windfall apples on the courthouse lawn.
They inhabit whatever margins we leave for them
completely. You want to follow
the deer's spoor as far as it takes you, a buck or doe
feeding quietly on browse. But your gaze could scarcely be
much different than that of the bank manager,
the owner of the hardware store, squinting
through the scope of a high-powered rifle,
lining up the crosshairs. Predator, lover, devourer,
maybe it isn't too late for you to learn
to keep your distance and love
something you must not touch.

Notes on Crows

They roost, ridiculous and sublime
in the old birch trees behind the house.

They've had a long day: mobbing the neighbour's
orange tabby crawling on her belly

through the long grass, eating the ass
out of a road-killed skunk, haute cuisine.

The teenager whose bedroom window
faces onto the backyard and the birches

isn't here now as dusk settles like volcanic ash.
It'll be after midnight when he stumbles home

drunk on a school night, four tries before his key
fits in the door. Early next morning, crows

will wake him from a fitful sleep. He'll consider
buying a pellet gun from Canadian Tire.

Loitering in the treetops, they are
every dumb mistake he's ever made.

So many it's a wonder the branches hold them.

LOYALIST BURIAL GROUND IV

Ever since you quit smoking, you don't know what to do
with your hands. When a group of teenage girls lights up,
the voice in your head says screw the Surgeon-General.
What harm could it do you now with your body's
routine infidelities? Spare tire, trick knee.
The girls are joined by a boy in baggy jeans, hooded
sweatshirt. They stand around talking, one girl
leans against a monument, another trails her hand absently
along the smooth stone. The boy starts to goof around,
feeling pent-up in his skin. Maybe
you should stop staring—*Okay, mister,*
let's get those hands up where we can see 'em.
But you couldn't drag your eyes away if you tried.
The tall skinny boy with the shaved head
is so in love with the dark-haired girl he can't
hide it, her distant smile keeps him up at night.
Your one wish is that they love each other simply
and fiercely for as long as it lasts. It's getting late,
dusk settling in the trees, shadows slanting from headstones.
The girl with the dark hair has someplace to go.
She starts walking, and what choice does he have
but to follow, the star of her cigarette pointing the way.

Alayna Munce

Degan Davis

Alayna Munce grew up in Huntsville, Ontario, and has spent most of her adulthood in the Parkdale neighbourhood of Toronto, where she spends her time writing and working in bars and community centres. Her work has appeared in various Canadian literary journals and has three times won prizes in *Grain* Magazine's annual Short Grain Contest. In 2003 she won second prize in the CBC Literary Awards' travel writing category. She has attended the Banff Centre's Writing Studio for both poetry and fiction.

To Train and Keep a Peregrine You Cannot Miss a Day

If, in the morning, I wake first, I lie awhile beside you.
A small window holds a square and impossibly partial
view: the outside world as seen from our bed, a scrap of sky
criss-crossed by the swaying upper branches of a dying
elm. Occasionally a bird. Lying there I gather evidence
of the day's weather. It was from you that I first heard

of bards whose minds were strong-benched ships, holds
full of heroes, well-tended hives aswarm with heroes; who,
in their apprenticeships, spent days fasting and prone, tartans
swaddled round their heads and head-sized stones
upon their stomachs while they mazed the many-branched
corridors of ancient stories and memorized the honeycomb, the
stroke
      stroke
           stroke of a thousand years. We leave each other
and return. Planets in syncopated orbits. Remember
that first winter we lived together? You worked days and I,
nights (me serving bottomless cups of black coffee to
cab drivers and drag queens at an all-night diner near
Maple Leaf Gardens, my name tag crooked; you
serving soup-kitchen slop to buddy who'd follow it up with a
cocktail in the park—can of Sprite spiked with aftershave—
unless you spared him a five for a real bottle, the tongues
of your untied workboots panting all afternoon in the dish room).
We both concentrated all we were on that hour near dawn
when I crawled into bed beside you—first hour of your day,
last of mine—that hour
      we overlapped. That hour
           yawned wide. Laughing, half
proud, we used to say, *Like ships passing in the night.* Later
we warned each other with phrases like, *to drift apart.* Still
later, a month of your face so foreign I knew you had forged
some strange alliance, yielded to the need for mutiny.
           We lose each other
and return. Now, our agendas let us curl in bed together,
though one of us always falls asleep first, leaving the other
stranded, beached in wakefulness. (There's no betrayal

greater than unconsciousness.) In the morning,
if I wake first, I lie awhile beside you, lie there memorizing
the verses of our life so far. Some mornings we are as
obsolete as an oral tradition. Other days, leaning
on the phrasing
                    of the moments
                                        of return,
I want to make and keep a promise,
master a forgiveness as ingenious and out of date
as the art of falconry.
To train and keep a peregrine
you cannot miss a day. Today
I want to say, *Every day*
at sunrise, love,
I will remove
the ornamented hood
                    and send the bird out
                                        to bring me
back.

WHEN YOU SAY HUMAN DO YOU MEAN IT

There's a man who travels
the sidewalks of my neighbourhood
in a wheelchair pulled by huskies.
I see him often at intersections,
three dogs panting, waiting
for the light to change.
At the exact moment it turns
green they spring
forward so if you didn't know better

you'd be confused
(do they trigger the light
or the light,
their movement?).

They pass the dishevelled man who stands,
barefoot in undone sneakers no matter what
the weather, one leg of his track pants
lodged up around his shin,
the other, ragged
under his heel.
He stands at the same
intersection all day long,
conducting traffic,
urging the cars forward and back
in perfect unison with the traffic lights.

This, perhaps, is as likely as anything else to
turn out to be
what makes the world go around.

The man in the wheelchair calls *yee* and *haw*
for right and left,
speaking the same language
my grandfather spoke behind his plough horses
once upon a time.

As they glide away
you can almost hear
the earth turning in response,
the *shshsh* of sled runners over snow;

can almost bear
to call the city home.

Someone has tapped a maple tree
in the parkette down the street
I think now I'll be able to sleep at night knowing
somewhere nearby there is an apartment,
windows fogged with steam—

                              shshshsh

—when it's all boiled down there will be just enough
to fill a teacup,
a bird's nest,
a bell.

One garbage day
my neighbour Bonnie
spotted an old leather couch on the curb
on her way to trade in her empties—
the springs in the couch were
shot so she skinned it.

Bonnie is Ojiibway,
makes dream catchers
with couch leather and seagull feathers
dyed eagle.

I'm standing at the intersection, waiting
for the streetcar. I see her pass with her bundle buggy,
waving. I wave back aware

I'm only human but hoping I have
the human touch. When you say the word
human do you mean it
as excuse or incantation? Ask me

and I am torn
between the two,
again and again my head
turned by how we make
do   on the way
to trade in
our empties.

THE YOUNG WOMAN'S THOUGHTS WHILE SQUATTING IN THE NIGHT GRASS TO PEE

what kind of prisms
do I have in me
that drink goes in me all colours
comes out always yellow
that error goes in me elbows
comes out winged
that injury goes in me sharp
comes out sculpture
that he goes in me hard
comes out human

George Murray

George Murray was raised in rural Ontario. He has also lived in Toronto, eastern Italy, New York City and Guelph. His poetry collections are *Carousel* (Exile, 2000), *The Cottage Builder's Letter* (McClelland & Stewart, 2001) and *The Hunter* (M&S, 2003). He has been nominated for a Pushcart Prize and won the gold medal for "Best Writing" in the New York Festival's International Radio Awards—the first time it has been won for poetry. George is also the father of Silas Kinton Jack Murray and the husband of Ailsa Craig.

Ailsa Craig

THE CARNIE'S OBITUARY

Dead in a Ferris wheel crash at forty-three, he was laid
below an overpass by the highway, clad as he would
have wanted in his best: rattlesnake boots, jeans,
a leather vest, two arms full of green dragon tattoos;
& they had an open casket as the cars whizzed by
above, brought balloons, pink clouds of candy floss
sticky pinwheel lollies, shabby red darts
with bent flights, a string of flashing marquee bulbs
with patio-lantern covers, and orange tiger on a leash;
& in a moment of silence from the bullhorns, the bells

of the carousel, the speeding traffic, his will was read,
the inheritance handed out: for each a Throwing Ring,
a single chance to toss a winner, to circle his head
in a rubber halo & help him bluff his way into heaven.

BLAZON FOR THE CRONE

For a skeleton there is a spinning wheel over which she is pulled;
for a heart there is a bucket, a well, a rope—

Her mind, a covered bridge, lets each memory rattle like
loose wood planks, grow in the corners like spider webs—

She is older than either paint or harebell, lime-ancient:
tuskless, yet still able to paw sand in anticipation—

Invisible inside, there is a curved retina, a fingertip's blunt
nerve ending, an eardrum pulled tight as embroidery—

Outside, her world is a tongue with tastebuds numerous as
strawberry seeds
                through which she moves like a glacier of salt.

EMBLEM

Listen: the mantis on the flower opens
her mandibles and waits, a frozen war emblem.

There was barely time to touch the surface
with a stone awl, much less scratch a name.

The games these Masons play: burying jars of milk
by the river against some war too secret to tell.

Speak: everything opined of the end
will be true, if only in that moment's outcome.

When seen moving through the dust motes
and the rotating fan's flickering shadow,

even the grass leaves muddy tracks, breaking camp
and marching an endless, singing army out to combat.

THE BATS

As the lakeside cottage slips into the plum of dusk,
the fir trees and cedars darkening the rocks,

mosquitoes and bats rise with the moon,
silhouetted over the deck in brief bursts,

black wings against a sky like the deepest vein—
and in the deck chairs below, cottagers pull sweaters

up around reddened necks, roll pant legs down
over fishing-wet ankles—

city-folk, convincing themselves after a day casting
on the shore that they are simply unsure

of the chill in a northern summer evening, or suspicious
of the hidden whine of insects, or taking

sensible precautions against sparks from the fire—
but truly it is a doubt of what intentions beat above,

the clicks like those of a disapproving tongue,
the sweeps and dives into the airspace

about their heads, the occasional brush of leather
against an exposed scalp—

it is some instinct to duck and cover
they're learning to use, a natural tendency to make

their jugulars scarce, to pull heads down
between shoulders even though

everything they've learned tells them the predators above
are only feeding on what's feeding on them.

Window

Close that time-frosted window with a stone,
close his mouth with your fist.
That dumb brute Samson was able to silence

the Philistines, why can't you? There comes
a point for all well-loved walls
when the number of hangings, past and present,

meet in an equation determining
structural integrity,
each nail biting into the wood boring out

its own little birth canal until the wall itself
resembles a senseless honeycomb
and the next nail has nowhere to go

but into the spackled cavern left
by one gone before. Here,
where attraction intersects with admiration,

here is where we spend our time
and call it love. Only now
after so many years have passed can we be sure

what the next season will bring. The gods
bathe in our flesh and we receive
and store their cast-away filth. Now,

come to think of it, this holds true
for well-hated walls as well:
each peephole, each suppurating bullet hole,

each angry fist. Sure, she cut his hair
but he was balding anyway.
It is hard to assign blame in situations

such as these.
It's hard to tell the windows
from the stones, the eyes from the bullet holes.

Jada-Gabrielle Pape

Aubrey Applewood Nealon

Jada-Gabrielle Pape is Coast Salish from the Saanich and Snuneymuxw Nations. She has a BFA in Creative Writing and a Master's in Education, both from the University of British Columbia. Jada works as a First Nations School Support Worker for the Vancouver School Board and writes as the sun comes up over her garden.

IMAGINE A HOME

with a core built like an anorexic's body:
starved deliberately
disappearing slower than the eye can detect

on the outside
a polite neighbour tells you
the paint job looks great

on the inside the meat wastes away
strands of sinew separating
from the skin until only bile stews
in a shadow, a memory, a whisper

or anything else too thin to stop
the whole frame from caving in on itself
imploding into its own blue-eyed reflection in the mirror

THE WAY MY JEANS GOT SHORTER

I pull and stretch the long cotton of my jeans
this year's hippest style—deliberately faded
in all the right places   you joked when
I first wore them—*did you get dragged behind a truck?*
we laughed at fashion
and when our sense of it would end

I lift the weighted garment from the washing machine
untangle it from wound-up arms of late winter shirts (twist)
pack the creaking basket back up the stairs
it doesn't matter what you're doing
you will always
take a moment to stand in front of me
pull the hemline of my pants   wet cotton in our hands
cold from the rinse cycle

we make faces as we pull
I almost see my pants growing
standing three feet from you
how can laundry day still be fun after all these years?

the day you moved out
shelves, boxes and suitcases

piled high in the living room
full of the clothes we picked out together
years of road trips   movies and love letters
in the middle of the house we built four years ago
in the winter—drywall dust in our hair
paint remover in our lungs—we ordered in every night
to the sound of the Nagano Olympics in the background

this year it wasn't Salé and Pelletier
that brought tears to our eyes
but spring in our garden
we threatened to lay down sod
to even out the bumps
but we never quite got around to it

now you live a block away
because we ran out of steam:
we're doing really well we're still best friends
we walk our dog together every day
but I haven't shared
with anyone   not even you
how I crave your smell and the touch
on the top of my head when you lean in
to kiss my scalp   I keep dear to me
your way of sneaking a sour candy
into my hand as you walk out from the corner store

and today   as I tried to stretch
the long cotton of my jeans
my arms even fully extended
couldn't meet the length or carry the weight

of this cold damp garment
I thought this is what is left of us
and found myself hoping
shorter pants will come back into style
and that I won't be too old to succumb to the trend

WHAT YOU ARE NOT
for Allan McEachern

we have ancestors
woven into the land
memories nestled in rock
beds of oceans and mountains
we have skin the colour of river clay
we have songs carried on heartbeats

we have columns of statistics that back up
like a septic tank on a hot summer day
all over newly planted grass
fresh shoots pushing up out of dark packed dirt
each one like a finger print or a topographical map

it is my mother who puts down roots
lets them spread deep below
the earth that will later house her body
amongst the stories of our ancestors

my older brother paves the way
for me and our future generations
his voice brings me home
if I start to think like you

the colonizer he says
will always be your oppressor
and you have given in to him
when you start to carry the burden of his anger
it is then
that he has won

and so I tell myself
more than I am telling you
you are not like me
I am not like you and you
have not defeated us

Alison Pick

Degan Davis

The title section of Alison Pick's book *Question & Answer* won the 2002 Bronwen Wallace Award for Poetry and the 2003 National Magazine Award for Poetry. The manuscript won the 2002 Alfred Bailey Manuscript Prize and the book was shortlisted for the 2003 Gerald Lampert Award. She has published and read across the country. Alison grew up in Kitchener, did her undergrad at the University of Guelph, spent time writing in Saskatchewan and now lives in St. John's. Her first novel is due out in Spring 2005.

WINTER: LEAVING THE FARM

This is the fall. It is spent.
Let us watch it depart like the red
flatbed truck on the horizon, kicking up

dust. Not speed but sureness
makes the road rise, lends the illusion
of motion. Do you hear me? I'm saying

it takes almost nothing to make gravel fly.
Kiss me. Again. Because the valley between us
in bed is wider than we dreamed

and growing. And new snow is building. Let us
stand in the wind with our throats tipped back, waiting
for the first flake to fly. Meet me at the barn,

its door swinging wide on its hinge like an answer
unexpected. Like yes. We'll ride the John Deere
to the centre of the field where the cow's breath will warm

your hands. My poor heart will break. I will
sing you every love song I can think of while pulling
the last of the beets, blood red, which we'll take

to the cellar where jars wait like feelings on the shelf.
Sealed off. A harvest of rhubarb, crabapples, pickles,
preserved. A feast for the winter. As if

the word *blessed* was to be saved.
Or *road*. The one with the pickup truck
leaving in dust: let that road carry us home.

QUIDI VIDI

Walk as far as you can,
then farther, past
the chain-link barring the road,
tire tracks deep as the rut of your mind,
the place you always get stuck.
Wanting more, or wanting
less, to be rid of the word
called wanting. Boulders,

tall grass, shrubs you can't name,
birds you can't name,
the ocean. Being a stranger sneaks you through
the latch of language—briefly. Bottles, you know.
Condoms, you know. And the weight
of being human where other humans have been.
Back of the sea like one line of thought,
slight variation of foam at the shore
where artifice gives itself up. Farther out,
a ledge in the rock
as though attention might help. Turning
for home, hands in your pockets, night mists in
like animal breath, the black-brown shapes
of gathering mammals
bending to drink at the silent pool
of mind submerged in the mind.
If a gap in awareness exists, it's there
you might have slipped through.

"Is it raining where you are?
Are you watching? Is the rain the story now?"
    – Helen Humphreys

How the rain falls. How
it fills the dusk with its sound,

buckets, pails, brown clay flower-
pots rising. How it lasts. How

the umbrella, motionless bird,
stands on one leg by the door. How

you get wet. How the rain runs down
the back of your collar, spills off

the slope of your nose. How it is gentle
and clean. How it is enough. How,

by the window, the rain is the story
that belongs to you more than any other.

How you sleep with its song
on the roof, blankets tucked under

your chin. How you snore. How the rain
makes a shelter of wetness, how it gives birth

to the river, then rests. How it hangs off
the raspberry bush, delicate lace

of the fern. Promising nothing
and keeping its promise, how the rain comes

to the edge of your sadness. How
it doesn't lie. How it doesn't judge. How

it is not afraid to cry.

Dreaming Easy

The final snow-removal trucks
arrive like liberating troops. Up and up
the streets they sail to roses thrown
from roofs. Winter's a storm window, gone.
This is clairvoyance, this single pane lifted,
light just beyond what's always been there,
the headiest, sweetest unseen. These are the days
of pre-cognition when memory reverses and
time speeds up—the uncombed hair
of the summer willow is more than a shelter of dream.

Dreaming is easy in hours like these,
pavement damp with growth and ferment,
but troops are troops, red-petalled or not.
And still I haven't said what I mean:
time is a ghost in the children's garden
trailing her hem in the dirt. Or,
what's unbroken isn't healed but only stitched back up.
Ice in the harbour, for instance, returned
to shadow the meaning of spring. The Quakers,
for instance, who worship the silence that empties
the outline of words. The shattered things, which is to say
the cool of your palm against my thigh, which is to say
there is no saying for human despair or desire. There is no
perfection. My broken parts have always been broken—
touch me. Touch me there.

Steven Price

Esi Edugyan

Steven Price was born and raised in Colwood, BC. His work has previously appeared in journals including *The Fiddlehead, Grain* and *Canadian Literature*. He has degrees from the University of Victoria and the University of Virginia, where he was awarded the Henry Hoyns Fellowship. A sequence of his poems was shortlisted for *Poetry* Magazine's Ruth Lilly Award in 2001. He recently completed his first manuscript of poems, *Anatomy of Keys*, a sequence about the life of Harry Houdini. He currently teaches poetry at the University of Victoria.

from *Anatomy of Keys*

VII

Such newsreels flicker still. Houdini's mother
watches crowds gather like a soot railing of crows.
A crawling steel bridge; ten thousand necks and the stretch

of girders toward a stinking canal. Her son's linked wrists.
The wet thump of flashbulbs as he smashes the water,
brown head gone in a looping circle of foam,

thick floods of bottom-mud below. The surface of the river
rolls shut like a desk; on either side factories block sun, blacken
water. Both dockyards hush. A thing he does to himself—

> but Ehrie was never a child, only smaller: in a peeling apartment
> in Appleton his elbows grind the lip of a tub, one finger crooks
> the shy hairless fish of his sex, he grins *Ma look at this!*

> and scrunches his nose, is gone quick as breath, heels farting
> the bottom and hair a sticky mess above him. Her darning clatters
> over tiles, oily silence—she recalls it still—her webbed lungs

> draining like weeds or yellow lake-scudge; a clot fills her ears
> loud as a river in the pores of a girl, her fast plaited river
> of Budapest, of childhood; she lunges, cries *Nein, nein Ehrich*—

his nose blowing careful air and him pausing
beneath the bubbling trail of pockets just long enough
to draw out the awe in her dark face.

XV

   The stories keys could tell,
still, of the rusted throats of cells, skeletal keys,
and keys knuckled like fingers, keys harsh-voiced
and stunned like a blaze of cold bells, copper keys,
birch keys, keys reeking of mulch and wet moss,
more, the excellent French names of keys, all eager
thigh, fluid, stamen, fumbling at locks themselves,
the tongue another muscular key at my lips, slipping

free, for I was careless, Bess, careless with such keys,
keys to trunks, chests, desks, keys choked in my gut
or wedged under nails, fang-toothed keys, and keys
drowned in jars like small dark snails, consider
the stubborn silences of these, what stories
they could tell; Bess, even this band on my finger
shines, a key.

XIX

– from Proverbs of Escape

The torn rope is twice useful.
A chained wise man remains free. A chained fool, escapes.
In old age even the butter-lid grins.
Lies of the illusionist; truths of the illusion.
The thickest cords fray fastest.
The tied trunk never tells the rope what it holds.
Where conscience is the door, privilege is the hinge.
When he is bound, the crowd is; when he is free, the crowd is not.
The fettered man's curses open only his own mouth.
In the Garden the key is no place. In Hell the key is every place.
God goes unnoticed. Satan goes hidden.
Shackled at daybreak, shadows. Shackled at dusk, lanterns.
No release without first being bound.
Skinniest wrists, hungriest cuffs.
Locks laugh not; weep not; but embrace all things with ease.
Knowledge into goodness. Wisdom out of goodness.
The new pick bends, the old pick breaks.
Mourning unties no knots. Praying unclasps no cuffs.
He who conceals everything conceals nothing.

Never how it was done. Always how it was not.
Compassion. Attention. Praise. An anatomy of keys.
To leave the self is love.

XXXIX

Squelch and slub of shovel blade.
All day rain-bloated ditches made
digging difficult, it floated spades,

it foamed up flecks of rotted pine;
a sogged gravesite, gushing long lines
of the haggard, granite dead. In time

rain gattles all tombs: Father's grave,
bundled in tarps, gave and gave,
a gash we floundered in to stave

off flooding. Then a blade slit wood.
Clumped half-sunk in a soft hood
of coffin. Sifted its stew of mud,

of flayed worms; harder things. His teeth.
All bilge and reek of meat and death.
Foul seepage. Like a long-held breath,

this, the harrowing of my father's
sacred bones, nails, ribs from earth;
to lift, exhume, return interred

those bits of him not led to God
in an Exedra I'd built our blood,
tall Greek marble, his left ribs laid

alongside Ma's. Shirred in that pit
the hired man tightened, held his lips,
fumbled deep a dreeped casket grip

and groped beneath. I threaded him
a rope, winched it firm: that coffin
slucking noisily clear, reeling in

and of a piece. Faith too is like that,
he'd believed; a thing hauled hard, set
to rights, a steady raising of the dead.

LI

Then the world's ropes untied themselves and it was understood
how much men relied on being bound; ships unmoored; crates fell
open; the tongues of shoes gloped sloppily out. The only sound a
soft, dull sump like wet snow. Not quite November. The world's
ropes untied and in untying bared a gulf that had been growing for
some time, a gulf within the world and not without. Even scarves,
being a kind of rope, slid mournfully from coat hooks and hangers.
Everywhere the relaxing of ropes forced a tensing of muscles. As if
to remind what is not borne by one is borne by another. All this in
an instant, like a sigh, before the knots flexed back; before the reptile
stillness of the ropes resumed. So intimate, men who did not smoke
found themselves fumbling for cigarettes, and secretaries who did

smoke merely stared mournfully at typewriters. So unexpected, schoolchildren were let from class to wade brown, sober sidewalks of leaves. So brief—and on this all were agreed—it might not have even happened.

XVI

Rope:
   sleek sash cord, escapologist's skin,
      umbilical of the drowned, woven shroud
hanged men bladder and drag and stretch out in;
wildfire ripple of rumour through a crowd;
sheath, frayed bloodline, sinew of fire and flint:
      asleep in one's lap like a child or a cat
and like a child all ululation, all wailed lament;
rope like a brambled path, leading both in and out;
      elbow; cut tongue; black intestine or spleen:
      dark many-cornered flesh a knot can be.
A kind of thread and weft we work behind,
what binds us and unbinds us, God to man:
Holy of Holies, spell, hand, prayer, shine:
      the shaking of my father's hands in mine.

Matt Rader

Melanie Willson

Matt Rader grew up in the Comox Valley on Vancouver Island. He is the publisher of Mosquito Press and co-founder of Crash: Vancouver's Indie Writers Fest. He studied writing at the University of Victoria and the 2003 Banff Writing Studio. He lives with his wife Melanie in Vancouver.

Exodus

6 p.m., March 17: My parents climb into my father's year-
old Ford pickup and drive the lake road down the Malahat
to Wayne Brown's place in Shawnigan Village.

My mother is fat and nervous and spends the evening
holding her belly in the corner of the kitchen, sprawled
on an old leather chair the Van Barneveld boys stole
from the Mill Bay Inn (just picked it up and walked out),
while Wayne and my dad drink a couple of Luckies
and smoke a j- on the back porch. It's warm

for mid-March. There's a housefly on the kitchen table.
The oven door is open. My mother wants to fall
asleep, she will later tell me, just curl up and go
inside herself, kick my ass into the world. She
is sure I am a boy, the way I will not leave her

body. "Today," she tells Wayne's wife Deirdre, "is my
Grandfather Langley's birthday." "Today is the day
they drove the snakes out of Ireland," says Deirdre,
and they both laugh, knowing full well it isn't

true. The men don't come inside all night. They piss
in the yard and when Mum asks for a ride home
they let Deirdre help her out to the truck.

Dad drives and Wayne sits in the middle. Mum
rolls down the window. They listen to Woody Guthrie
sing "1913 Massacre" and part of "The Biggest Thing
Man Has Ever Done" before the truck ruts
on the shoulder, blows out the right front tire.

There are no street lamps on the lake road, no moon
above the trees. Dad curses the corroded flashlight
batteries. There is the smell of manure and fresh water.
My mother gets out of the truck, places her hands on
the hood, fingers the dirty heat from the engine.

Tonight, I am due to be born. There are headlights
coming towards us. Mum sticks out her thumb.
"Hang on Baby," she whispers "we're almost home."

FALLING

Clipped my skull on the lip of the bridge
as I plunged feet-first into the anxious river.
My teeth jawed together, all castanet
or clamshell, crunched my tongue to pulp.
I couldn't talk, or scream, or lift a finger.
Couldn't remember why I was there or where
amongst all the falling my body had gone.
Rivulets of red ribboned my head like an insect-
painter's quick study of the wingless human—
The Faller—a gesture-drawing in blood and air.
Here's how I picture it: limbs all stutter and wheel
in the rioting wind, all seizure of sign language
and panic-dance, eyes scrolled back, calculating
velocity by distance, the time left to swallow
or spit before impact. Never mind the fear
or embarrassment, I pissed my pants just for
the warmth in my crotch, that one last sloppy kiss.
Falling and falling is lonely business.

PREPARATIONS

Broke the bird bath with a sledgehammer before the sun
got up and spent the rest of the morning draining
the goldfish barrel and burning it in the firepit. Have to
wonder what viruses or spores, what bugs
were borne off with the smoke or survived buried
in the ash and coal, gone dormant, but alive,
violent and unpredictable as volcanoes. Still,

we do what we can. Used to be
the crows were so noisy I couldn't sleep past seven.
Now silence is the thing that wakes me—the birds having been
poisoned or exposed, infected with a new blackness
that caused them to lose contrast, I guess, and disappear.
So it's an end to standing water in the backyard.
An end to composting the robins that storm
against the kitchen window, played by the wind
for a joke, an offering or omen laid crooked
and limp at the foot of the house. No more
evenings on the front porch reading or watching
the children skateboard or ride bikes in the street;
nights we go indoors to avoid the bugs and spray trucks
that roam the neighbourhood like ghosts
from the days of chemical warfare and plague.
Later today, I'll go down to the lake to count ducks—
some now turning up dead in the reeds—
the numbers used to track the disease as it deepens
and spreads species to species. Other volunteers
bag the bodies and take photographs
as if at a crime scene. For me it's an excuse
to get away from the house, to put my mind to use—
condition my memory for field and forest of the future,
for clearing or lakeshore, where all the fliers are
gone and only imperfectly remembered.

RIVER VIEW

You leave the house and walk
towards the water. The city you live in
is built on floodplain and farmer's field,

flat as the ancient world, when all was balanced
on the shell of a turtle. The land you walk is
below sea level, yet the road slopes
towards water. All log boom and tugboat,
small fingers of wood, you fix the river's shape
in your mind, its glassy mathematics,
how it happens so quickly,
paced between hummingbird and midnight.

The clammy spill of moon on your neck,
like a blade laid flat against skin.
You're all goose-pimple and runny nose
as you stroll the quay. You stop
and stars swim like mackerel into your pupil.
Kneel and tie your sneaker.
For a moment you wonder why you are here
and not at home, in bed with your lover.
You begin to remember,
I left the house and walked towards the water . . .
You begin to remember,
then you forget,

steal a dinghy from a ship
called *It's Real*, and row into the river,
eyes shut, pulling away
from the shore. Apartment lights
leak through your eyelids.
You heard the word
and it sounded like *river.*
I left the house and the boat's taking on water . . .
You hear it now.
Row harder, it says. *Row harder.*

FAITH

Stored Dad's ashes in a mason jar—
swept them from the funeral pyre
after it cooled, bits of bone and tooth,
the smell of salmon somehow.
Kept him in the living-room
fireplace and had no more fires.
Tried not to look during breakfast.
Looked. Duct-taped the glass,
then peeled it off before Mum saw.
I wanted to make him an hourglass,
my sisters thought a pillow or shaker,
someone said beach. At night
I stole pinches of foot, dashes
of hand, refilled it with sand,
and buried him toe-by-finger
in potted earth and rose seed.
In this way he came back to me:
root and thorn, rosehip, became
jam that smelled of fishmeal,
forty-one white petals I pressed
between the pages of my hand.

Shane Rhodes

Arion Predika

Shane Rhodes has published poetry, essays and reviews in magazines, journals and newspapers across Canada. He was born in Edmonton, Alberta and has lived in Calgary, where he received his BA in English; Fredericton, where he received his MA in English; Guanajato, Mexico; and presently resides in Ottawa. He has been an editor with *The Fiddlehead, filling Station* and *Qwerty*. Shane won the Alfred G. Bailey Award and the Alberta Book Award for his first collection, *The Wireless Room* (NeWest, 2000). His second book, *Holding Pattern* (NeWest, 2002) won the Archibald Lampman Award.

DAY AND NIGHT THE SEA WHISPERED THALASSA
for C. Creery

She called to say her mother had died
    earlier that day. In her voice there was
no quivering
    but solidity as from one who has found

the flaw in matter. Somewhere distant lilacs
    and purple thunderheads opening

over grasslands. The start of losing her
        was knowing what could be missed:

a movement of hand, snap-
        dragons in the window, a way
of occupying the gaps between the times
        she wasn't noticed—which are

lust, are presence, the one way time

finds its way home. She had promised the day before
        she would soon get better and so
the start of fiction.
        I can't remember what I said

but it was unimportant
        —language coiled
in silence as, on the coast,
        small pieces of glass worn by the sea

are called "angels' tears" for we think grief
        the permanent state of the godly. Sitting in a room
with the afternoon light falling through the window—
        which was everything between you and what you

wanted to get at—her mother's body grew cold
        as love can, as a thing being written about can.
Flowers on the table dropping white
        petals to the pastel rug, not losing them

symbolically but, as in real life with real flowers, one

by one. How quiet
    stillness
waits yet how ceaselessly
    we pursue it. How quiet. How helpless.

A smell in the room not of
    death but of things to be remembered:
hair over forehead, an empty glass
    of water. There are few

times we appear human enough
    for paintings but death is one of them.
I hope, she said to me, her voice over the telephone
    distant, as from one side of a wound

to the other, *I hope,*—the syllables
    coming down from the wire, dis-
mantling, as if *they*
    and *soon* and *her*

were sounds of another language
    that would have to be washed,
dressed and put to flame, the words
    becoming the body lying there now

dismantling protein, now a certain thickness
    of light as it digs itself out of colour, now
the unbeknownst heroine of a story she is
    instrumental to yet not a part of, separating, separating . . .

As if something was leaving, was

building its own ending apart from all of us—
        the imprint on the sheets, the verbs cooling down
into nouns already, into the body, spirit and breath
        which the Incas would draw

as scrolls of paper hanging before us
        all rolling up into an ending, now, more complete than
even the end of words or breath which,
        especially now, with the light lost in trees and snap-

dragons stubbing themselves out in the window, where even the
        notes, the early evening dew on grass, the spirit rising
with the thermals from the sun-baked ground, even the sky
        which has fallen, is falling, will continue

to fall, even the crumpled pieces of paper
        sown into the cuffs of jackets

        (especially the crumpled pieces of paper sown into the cuffs of
        jackets)

that Pascal called his *inimitable proof of god,* even that,
        burning off into denouement, into unending thrust, into funerals

and eulogies, into the cakes and sandwiches eaten
        after, after all, after that, after this, after
she said, *I hope,* and it need mean nothing more than
        itself, the simple need for finality, like one cleaning up

corn husks after a great meal, but it was more
    finished than even this or an ending could rightfully be,
I hope, she said to me over such long distance, *I hope*
    they soon come and get her.

from HAYNES TOWN STORE

                my grandmother and grandfather said
                      to my father said
                          to me said

—if you sat here long enough
you could count the population in an hour
using one eye and two hands and
if you sat here long enough you could
do the post-mortem best to start at the curling rink
and move on to the outdoor skating rink and the
catholic church all disguised as the heart but the store
and the layers of tobacco spit on the floor and while
well I don't know for sure but somebody
must have 'whittled' here once if you sat here long enough
then must have been here even before the first train
hit the last cree crossing the main street and the
last mastodon lost itself between the coke machine and
the erratic chevy the other side of the pleistocene
if you sat here long enough, the store was there
before, I'm sure—

                my grandmother said

—he comes from the southeast coast of china as a boy
(or a man or as far as I can figure out
wing wong was a hundred all his life)
and after two months on ship or so it is said
in vancouver he buys a pound of chocolate
and after two months of rice and saltwater
it tasted of tears   wing speaks no english yet
he has selling in his blood like the last dime in his pocket
he buys more chocolate and breaks it to ten pieces
and sells each piece to the immigrants off the boats
for 5¢ each to people like wing or you or me hungry for land
or anything that looked like dirt and tasted like the dust storm
wing bought his store with
and a bag full of nickels—

                                                        but, I said

—why would he settle here
on this spur-line clot of grain dust and
sedimentary white puritanism there must be a billion
such towns joined together by clay silica rail
and conjunctions like some nervous system waiting
for wing to look out the train window at the red deer
river valley and say he saw a city in twenty years
the land he would buy for pennies and sell for thousands and
what else wing you crazy chinaman they asked *what else do you see*
wing wong says *a store* and they laugh as he touches the map
with a piece of chocolate and grinning says *here*
the store will be here—

matt robinson

Greg McMullen

matt robinson was born in Halifax and currently lives in Fredericton, where he works in Residential Life at the University of New Brunswick. He has a BA and BSc (St. Mary's), a BEd (Mt. St. Vincent), and an MA (UNB). His collections include *tracery & interplay,* a letterpressed limited edition of hockey poems from Victoria's Frog Hollow Press, *how we play at it: a list* (ECW) and *A Ruckus of Awkward Stacking* (Insomniac), which was shortlisted for the Gerald Lampert and ReLit Poetry Awards. The recipient of awards such as the Petra Kenney International Poetry Prize and the New Brunswick Foundation for the Arts' Emerging Artist of the Year, robinson is Poetry Editor at *The Fiddlehead* and President of the League of Canadian Poets.

F(X)—5TH METACARPAL; ON SEEING THE X-RAY
OF YOUR BROKEN HAND

at first: the suspension of
disbelief. then, comparison—the compulsion

to equate it, this image's spectral nonsense, with something
else; to make it lithographic, reproducible.

and so: try fog taking shape, playing at
       art, that night on the way back

       from the party when you were drunk, but not
       too drunk, and near the sharp still

       decline of the water's edge
       traipsing the gravel road that lined it: the less

       populated end of the harbour. that's what it's like. or,
       perhaps, the shape and seeming

       density of exhaled desire (a sheer
       fuel spewing: leaked from

       wherever, whatever it is, inside you that
       has burst) breathed onto

       the windshield in the cramped boudoir of a father's '88
       accord. that, on the night when, although you'd deny

       it quicker than the split that
       was your first time, it's the nervous december

       air outside, not you, that does that
       to her nipples. yes. these both and more; other

       memories, too, share
       something—resemblance, congruency—with it,

       the cloudy scaffolding they insist is
       simply your hand.

but these, however, are the facts: the knuckle—on
the film, in your hand—is displaced,

fractured and away from its normal metacarpal
syntax. and the twinge, the

dull ache: these are instruments of artifice. all
bits or pieces awash in their

respective museums, fleshy or synaptic; broken or
discarded—adrift—in that

sticky—sometimes sweet, sharp—human cocktail.

PITCH; (LOVE POEM FOR THE MONTREAL EXPOS)

      between the wind-up (the elaborate cat's
cradle tangle, its sinewy

coiling which, among other things, nearly—no, *surely*—
defines foreshadowing without

the use of any words, any language
other than that joint and

tendon syntax of our flesh), between that and the ashen
crack of bat or dust-echoed snap

of leather (those finalities or
possibilities), this, all of it. the sun. the questions about

the phone bill, the cable—overdue? the way she
turned in her sleep last night; how

he'll tell her, or, not tell her. and the right-fielder,
his wife. how she seemed a step, a

hand, *something* too friendly at their last
awards thing, although it could have simply been the beer,

nothing else. further, the now
sudden synthetic grey snugness of the pitcher's ball

pants and his, too—*yes, his!*—and does that (he's read
about this) make him gay? all this. and the sun. that

sun: the heat, the glowering immediacy
of it; how the ball, how what should be the ball right

there screaming headlong toward him, is nowhere—
everywhere—a million dark spots—all

those shadows—strobe-dancing, cutting across his eyes.

NOTES TOWARDS AN APARTMENT STORY

                    it could begin, this sketch of
our basement building, with how

we—*in medias res,* my father
and i—emerge, day's-end ghosted with sprinklings

of plaster, scaling the back
stairs' green-carpeted well, my allergic dust-cough

hacking out the back door's failing, dusk-screened evening
light like a confused dog's

announcement of morning.   or
with the decision—we'll say it took place at

the dining room table (the bills, scattered shingles of mail, all
shovelled aside and coffee-

cup-pyloned)—with the graph-
paper pact to build the thing, to frame that space, at

all.   or maybe with no words, as such: simply the felt-
penned diagrams—the rasp shuffle

of paper; a father's near-silent geometry?   or,
perhaps, all things considered, it *should* begin after the fact.

start with the pine shelf, all
six-feet-by-three-feet-by-ten inches, varnished and still

there, these four years since i've moved from
the province, my brother's snapshots now tacked to its sides.

       but here's a thought: to begin—an appendix,
a catalogue of excisions, the things

we left others to do. like the plumbing
and wiring—the real guts of the chore, knowing full

well that was not our forte. knowing
too well that most things we do, whether we wish them or

not, become in the end a mere list of deferrals, a counting
of spaces. like leftover linoleum:

the spilt-shuffled tile puzzle of what's
been, been left, been left out: to stand, or to sit in a place.

A HOME ECONOMICS

        the apartment is a mess, flung and
filthy, really. and we are, for all intents and purposes, madly (as

they say) in love. the kitchen sink is harlequin: an off-kilter
reminder of our appetites—the tupperware all

jaunty with the flaking batter aftermath of
lazy pancakes and other such thinly veiled suggestions

of sex. even the drain proclaims this lust, its stopper loose
enough that the dishwater has spent itself dry and

fully out of the basin. the fridge sweats something earthy, almost
vegetive: not only preserving, but now

producing as well. look: a glance at the counter shows it
wet, spilt juice-slick and tacked with mail, some

envelopes weary—finger torn and ragged
—while others, still crease-and-fold new, wait for a tongue.

Laisha Rosnau

Robert Ahrens

Laisha Rosnau was born in Quebec and grew up in British Columbia's Okanagan Valley. Her poetry, short fiction and non-fiction have been published in journals and anthologies in Canada, the US and Australia and a limited edition chapbook of her poetry, *Getaway Girl,* was published by Greenboathouse Books in 2002. Her first novel, *The Sudden Weight of Snow,* was published by McClelland & Stewart in 2002. Her first book of poetry, *Notes on Leaving,* was released in 2004 by Nightwood Editions. Laisha currently lives in Vancouver.

POINT OF EXIT

Let us return then, to the bathroom
of Tim Hortons, the first equation
of inebriation—one two-sixer, three
girls, straight down. Let us return
to everything that followed, a night
like mercury—metallic taste
in mouths, figures nimbus-lined,
time a slow, smooth drop.

Let us return to where we lined up to enter
a community dance, too young then to understand
nausea, the room spun out, a wheel of sparks
off us, and all we could think was
Let it always be like this. Later, watch
as we drape over chairs, necks stretched
taut between weight of hair, heft
of hearts, as we each hold the smooth
beating fish of boys' tongues
in our mouths and we think, *It will be.*
It will be like this.

When you return with us there,
you will hear it—in the squeak
of our tight throats between words,
in the whistle of air we take into
our nostrils, pink-rimmed and dry,
in the knock of bones
when our knees have forgotten
which way is forward—you will hear:
We have to go now. Let's get out of this place.

ON THE GROUND

You are on a foam mat
in your best friend's basement, counting
to one hundred, slowly, wishing
you could skim off part of yourself.

You already know that certain women
can divide. Grade 11 Psychology

has taught you that some can split
from within, tear a twin out,

whole and invisible as an atom,
while the body waits, heavy
and tractable in hands that smell
of dirt, chalk, vinegar. Hands that press

silence like inky fingerprints into skin
until those girls and women split again—quavers
and semi-quavers rising up around their bodies,
humming to distract. You know all this

by the time he spreads your legs, puts his mouth
there. You wish you could hover near
the low ceiling, see the open legs and buried head
as just that—two limbs and a skull

—but you watch the television glow
on his shoulder, a sleek hump,
not from up there but from where
you are, on the ground.

CENTRAL STANDARD

We take turns showering, then neither of us
dry off, moisture our defence. We drip
prints around your apartment, thin slips
stick to us, first with water,
then with sweat.

I am not used to the heat, the time zone,
and you tell me to sleep in your bedroom
during afternoons, the fan filtering sounds
of kids calling from the schoolyard,
a slim street away.

The walls are tracked with wine-coloured
trails where you rolled paint, the sponge
prints still visible, giving everything
texture, closing like velvet
around me with the heat.

Your sheets are twisted, the night
sweat dry, the pattern of your lover
and you together erased with the code
of my own body, tossing. I sleep now
so that we can be awake together later.

When I get up, we go to the fire escape,
drink beer from wineglasses, tease the cat
with cigarettes. We each snag our vintage
bawdy house slips on rough parts
of the wrought-iron bars.

When your boyfriend comes home,
we call to him, show him our ripped
satin, tell him that when he goes out
for more beer, to bring back matches,
please. We aren't going anywhere,

and the night? It is young and we will
hold it right here, between us.

THE GIRLS ARE SLEEPING

The girls are sleeping, books splayed out
around them. Lips parted,
they take in air in quick small sips

like soda up a straw. I like to believe
they are innocent but I know how I am
around them, lips parted,

words held, hot frustration. Myself, age eleven:
tart candy stuffed on quick fingers into hip pockets.
They *are* innocent but I know how I was then

with bright girl lips and wide eyes, the knowledge that
I could attract anyone I wanted, slip them in
like tart candy stuffed on quick fingers into hip pockets.

My girls are sharp readers; I know
they find the good parts, laugh themselves asleep.
I can still attract anyone I want, slip them in

late, tuck them into my bed while I check to see if
the girls are sleeping, books splayed out.
They found the good parts, laughed themselves asleep,
taking in air in quick small sips.

David Seymour

Adrienne Barrett

David Seymour was born in Campbellton, New Brunswick, but grew up in Milton, Ontario, spending his summers in the Maritimes. He has since lived in Hamilton, Ontario, where he attended McMaster University and received a combined honours degree in English Literature and Philosophy; Edinburgh, Scotland; Fredericton, NB, where he received a Masters degree in English Literature and Creative Writing at the University of New Brunswick; and Rosarito Beach, Mexico, just south of Tijuana. Intermittent forays into the film industry have allowed him to keep afloat financially and to continue writing. He currently lives in Toronto.

INJURED SWAN, HIGH PARK

Your stillness is a disturbance,
cyclists and joggers stop to take a look.
A boy wades into the pond and lifts you out of the reeds.
His sister places almonds, bites of apple
on your wide back, rushes to their father in a fit of giggles
then gathers the courage to return and stroke your feathers.
You tolerate it all patiently, steadying the pain

with a casual grooming, careful not to brush
too closely to your unfurled left wing.

If everything were made of light
you would still have arrived first
and arranged yourself in the middle of things.
The whiteness of your body bends the afternoon around it,
like a childhood fever; airy cotton sheets,
cold face cloth, glass of water on the bed stand,
the whole room weightless, unfastened from its colours.
                              Like drifting, sourceless music
that tells the rest of us we are only half-formed,

accidental. I wait for you to raise your looped neck,
voice your disapproval and burst out over the water,
because, no, you shouldn't be here among us,
except that your broken wing
has made you heavier than air,
heavier, now, than ever.

PERLERORNEQ

 *– a Killinemiut word which, roughly translated, means
 'to feel the weight of life in winter'*

It is time to save the things
I might otherwise have thrown away,
leaves eddying around the trees
colour frozen in the vein, scarf of sparrows
winding through the empty branches.
At evening the sunlight strikes the houses sideways
like thinning blood. Children and shadows

quickly vacate the neighbourhood.
There is a point when animals,
badly confused, or simply
tired of homing, do not return but go
farther astray, like memory, farther north—Igloolik,
Tromso, Komolomec—become cold bones forgotten
under drift; winter's resolution. But I will grow
a fur of transparent hairs to collect
leftover light, a pot-belly, I will
practice reading in the dark, develop
a leanness of vision, clean past contour.
I will wander outdoors measuring each footstep.
Steadily the Arctic hares burrow into twenty-two
hours of nightfall, caribou taste the air;
they know wakefulness differently, know places
where no one wants anyone to be.

EARLY MORNING CITY

A low menace of clouds, a muffle.
The room we enter
when we sleep, its colony of empty seats,
the long corridors into the world, everything
gone missing.
                    I shift in bed
when the light falls,
like wet snow, on my shoulders
and my hair—
something has been torn,
a wound in the air, in the heart

a silence. The sky
congeals to a bruise.

All the cats in the city
are padding through the alleys
into other, paler darknesses.
And the stones of the older buildings
begin to grow in the grey half-light,
quietest and most alive.

from HEAD ARRANGEMENTS: TWELVE-STRING POEMS
FOR HUDDIE LEDBETTER

A sound on the wind wakes him, so he sneaks past Australia's pallet to the open window and peers out. The darkness around the log cabin is skin-tight, but for the odd flare of a burning stump the oxen can't root from the earth. Even the stars are gone. His mamma and papa are still somewhere in the fields clearing brush with uncle Terrell. Further off, as his eyes adjust, the low north sky brightens with the halo of a bonfire; a sukey jump at old Simms' farm. The oily smell of roasted peanuts and rabbit fat blows in gusts from that larger, fainter light. Holding the windjammer Terrell brought from Mooringsport, he strains for snatches of music above the mild din and echo, trying to mimic the melodies; faster than the church spirituals. The buttons aren't placed conveniently for a seven-year-old's fingers. Australia lies awake listening now, but doesn't say a word as her brother plays. One by one, the stump fires wink out. This gift from his uncle, all he owns.

I laid down last night, turnin' from side to side, I wasn't sleepin'—I was just dissatisfied.

He uses his voice as a beacon while Lemon stumbles, reaches for the sound, stumbles again, then with a sudden clear instinct heaves his great bulk onto the steps of the car as it retreats from the Dallas platform. Inside, the conductor sees their instruments and doesn't bother asking for tickets. By the next stop they've fangled a new ballad for the passengers. Their rendition of "Fare Thee Well, Titanic" begins to loosen purses. Lemon smiles—squint-eyed cherub face on the body of a grizzly—as quarters plink into the tin cup; he can tell when it's a nickel or a dime. During a break they sip whisky, talk about their wives, Lemon just nineteen and newly wed, wrestling, bootlegging. The train slips past Silver City, Waxahachie. Watching his new friend ride the neck of the half-empty bottle along his guitar strings, listening to the coiled steel twinge and complain. Like an old salvaged feeling. Dark as this starless night, those icy waters of the North Atlantic.

I'm sitting here wonderin', would a matchbox hold my clothes.

Loud and powerful as a well-made woman. An easy rider. Stella, the auditorium model. His first is painted green as a young cornfield, and so big the slightest touch sends a raw wow and shudder through the hollow belly. Mahogany back and sides from Honduras, German spruce top plate, American birch fretboard, rosewood bridges and inlay. Mixed pedigree; twice the size of Blind Lemon's Hawaiian. He buys it in Dallas second-hand for ten dollars; two thousand pounds of picked cotton. The action on the twelve, heavy-gauge steel strings is loose but difficult, the kind of jangle his ropy forearms have wanted to dance with for years. There is an avoided violence, a perfect artlessness in the chords—bass octaves running away with the croon in his voice. Or the poise of an arranged idea, as though he's heard this sound in his head all along and just needed to find its proper instrument. Outside, while he plays, the world's forest fires burn with abandon.

If yo' house catch afire an' dey ain' no water roun', throw yo' jelly out de window, let de doggone shack burn down.

Sue Sinclair

Lory Hall

Sue Sinclair grew up in Newfoundland, went to school in New Brunswick and currently lives in Toronto. Her first collection of poetry, *Secrets of Weather & Hope,* was shortlisted for the Gerald Lampert award in 2002. Her second collection, *Mortal Arguments,* was published by Brick Books in 2003, and a new collection, *The Drunken Lovely Bird,* is forthcoming from Goose Lane Editions. When not writing poetry or working at Book City, Sue puts on her dancing shoes.

SASKATCHEWAN

The cows have come
to see us, leaning
their soft, mucousy noses
over the fence, their breath
heavy and smelling
of the ocean—salt, mollusc,
seaweed—it's not difficult
to imagine them, hooves and horns
rising out of the waves. Testing
their footing, they clomp
up the beach and wander

out to the prairie, looking for a place
to lie down. Their eyes show
how far they have travelled
but not what they have
seen. They have the look
of all lost peoples:
everything, even intelligence,
submerged, they peer
at us, wait for us to make
the first move. Only at dusk,
near the salt lick, do they
reveal themselves. We overhear
their rough tongues scraping
the block, as if that
were the way home.

LYRIC STRAIN

The hum of bees. How it unnerves us: we tremble
when a tree branch bends too low. The din
of traffic is almost more bearable than the garden
where a hungering quiet erupts from the roots,
cell by vivid cell.

A bee hovers near, quivers in the shadow
of the ear. We stiffen, scared it might drop
inside and set our bones ringing. The sound is after all
not too large but too small: a resonance our skulls
can't bear. What we feared wasn't the great brightness
but the minute trembling
of tiny hairs, that shiver of recognition.

METROPOLIS

The city is a piano, its pedals sunk
deep underground. Commuters in the subway
listen to the instrument creak,
feel their own bodies shudder and give.

There is more memory here than we can manage.
We become paper shredders for obsolete decades—
strips of the past float down
like confetti from tall buildings, festoon the shoulders
of the unemployed. History will disappear entirely
if we work hard enough.

We all want the day to be our own.
Shoulders rub on shoulders. If everything else were silent,
it would sound like rain:
we are divisible by thousands and remain thousands.

DEPARTURE

Sometimes, autumn reveals the inward
light of things we call *glowing*.
A handful of red maple leaves.
A light that doesn't exceed itself
and has something to do

with departure. Think of a church,
the long, slow, sad colours, the way they linger,
miles from the sun, with no thought
of lingering. Again the red leaves.

Lay them on a table.
The dead have come back
to haunt the surface of the wood.
They can see themselves in the polish,
appear and disappear, something more than
and less than a face.

At the end of everything, you think,
there is this—this quickness,
this vanishing, this brilliance. The unseen
glimmer that bound it all together
escapes and is forgiven.

And everyone knows that forgiveness
gives off light, that healing
is the next thing to fire. It calls you
as it goes. You lay your
hand on the table.

CANOEING THE ST. JOHN RIVER

Reeds hover on the brink
of disappearing, lilies so white they're barely
present, child-like in their proximity
to the timeless.
                    As the light confesses
to impure thoughts, a lecherous heart, we listen.
It wants a verdict, something to call its own,
but we can only hear it out:
                                    at certain distances

we become helpless, image of the earth's
own helplessness. Things retreat so far
into themselves that surfaces seem evacuated.
We don't know what to make of what we see,
choices between equal uncertainties:
sky, water, lilies. Who knows if there's an inner life.

THE HIDDEN

Spring: the earth softens and sinks,
tugs us toward our wounds
but we're not brave enough,

can't let beauty
dig its spade deep into us,
to the place where our deaths
are buried.

Blue sky, light dripping
like water from an oar. The eyes
made of silver, as though they don't see
but reflect. It's too much for us:
the pressure of the changing season,
the new leaves struggling to unfurl.
We want to go away,
but can only drift further into the gaping mouth
of what we fear to name.

Nathalie Stephens

Photomaton

Nathalie Stephens writes in English and French, and sometimes neither. Born in Montréal, she grew up in Toronto and Lyon. Writing *l'entre-genre,* she is the author of *Somewhere Running* (Arsenal Pulp, 2000), *Paper City* (Coach House, 2003), *Je Nathanaël* and *L'INJURE* (l'Hexagone, 2003 and 2004). *UNDERGROUND* (TROIS, 1999) was shortlisted for the Grand Prix du Salon du livre de Toronto (1999). The recipient of a Chalmers Arts Fellowship (2002) and a British Centre for Literary Translation Residential Bursary (2003), Stephens has translated Catherine Mavrikakis into English and R.M. Vaughan into French. Some of her own work has been translated into Basque, Bulgarian, Portuguese and Slovene. On occasion she translates herself. She lives between.

from *Paper City*

Début

n and *b* were in their dictionaries when Art fell. *n* was *néant. b* was betwixt. Side by side and at times apart they were glutinous and unlawful. They were referred to in some circles as *necessary evils.* Circumscribed, disregarded, outcast. Scarcely tolerated. The folly ascribed to them served primarily to excise them, to render them *harmless* or *insignificant.*

We have been split at the hoof, n said. Where she went she left marks clippety-clop.

A tear down *b*'s face cleaved it in two.

A century ended one hundred years ago. *Plus ça change.* Demonstrably. A span of time is not equatable with years passed. We have new fonts if little else. The writing on the wall is illegible. *Le cri* is the echo of a drunken frat boy hitting the sidewalk. He lands face first in vomit, oblivious to the dissonance of fallen cities. While his friends identify chunks of carrots and evaluate the quality of bile, ancient walls *s'effritent* immeasurably.

The author is not positing *a better day.*

Merely we are watchful: *nous veillons.*

b produced *Commodify me.* How the Artists swooned! (They had forgotten irony.) Some heard *Come modify me.* They were doubly rapt. They dinned *b*'s *unexpected turnaround!* (Allowing this once for the *minuscule;* for hadn't he too, *enfin,* capitulated?) Indeed he was spinning. With impatience no doubt as *n* saw him off at *la gare.* He was boarding a train and *n* was seeing him off. The city grew impatient for that departure.

Everywhere artists were fucking. They were uncharacteristically immoderate. Art fell further. *n* and *b* grew silent. One waved a white hankie. The other brushed aside a tear. For they courted anachronism. Half-smiles. And the body's curvature as the train pulled out of the station. *n* tucked her soft cock into her skirt. This was no time for jubilation. *n* and *b* were in mourning. Each for the other and individually. The road was long across the ocean and neither had learned to fly outside of sleeping. They were suddenly wide awake. They were slipping from the page. Inconsolably.

From the start they had been unabashed *idéalistes*. They had entrusted their tongues to language and privileged labials over all other sounds. That is until they were confronted with *la langue*'s unmentioned parsimony. They were crestfallen, each and together, and both refused speaking, inevitably. The consequences were abysmal. *L'abîme* whispered *n* as she disappeared but not without shaking a fist. They were crossing themselves out of their city: *rayé,e,s*. They had cast themselves against the brashness of white, the flickering screen, the unwritten page, the frothing sea, the blinding snow.

n's last words, as *b* had recorded them, were inaudible.

As they slipped through the broken link of a twisted metal fence, they glanced back at nothing.

The contorted faces of the Artists turned skyward.

At the joining of two streets, a book caught fire. *b* put the match out with his tongue and fluttered his eyes.

The body is heat. Art is desire. Their city had altogether fallen.

from *Somewhere Running*

PLATE No. 9

Together   perhaps they are together   in and out of the image one stopping at a distance from the other   which would account for the absence of one   the one woman who appeared later   in the image   before the artist   who might not have noticed her presence   but they both   the women   the two women   both women are present from the beginning   inside and outside of the frame   the one that marks lines around the image   the one this image   in which two women   standing and leaning   one woman present   the other not   until later   until the artist shuddered   and the shudder   marked by the fissured city imprinted on the image   indicates the presence of two women together   one woman and then another   she   the woman they   the two women   leaning and standing within reach of the artist   and the need to readjust the line of vision   the one that draws one woman to the other   she   both   they   the two women   perhaps drawn one to the other   and maybe outside of the frame they are lovers,

Plate No. 14

They   the eyes that watch   see everything   the artist   the women   the frame   the hard ball forming   in the image that draws a line between two women   both leaning and standing at a corner in the city that fissures   and the pull   the eyes that watch notice the pull away from the frame   the line that pulls the two women outside of the frame   outside of the lines that fix two women in space and in time   and in the background a shudder all of this the eyes that watch see   and the pull also   the pull away from the image   into the small room with the window away into a conversation between the two women   somewhere else running and laughing   together or apart   laughing at the men who drop their pants   this the eyes that watch see   they are aware of two women's lives spilling outside of the frame and the streets that carry them away from the corner and the shadow into a small room or an alleyway   and there they are laughing both sitting and laughing   and the lean   one toward the other

in the small room   two women leaning and laughing   both
sitting on the floor or the chair or the bed   and the distance
there is little distance in the small bright room   between them
closing   becoming small   smaller than the small room   two
women sitting close in a small room   two lovers   women
close   one to the other   and the bright light through the
window against a dark sky and a candle perhaps   lit on the table
beside an open book   here in the room   the two women read
together   or one woman reads   from a book   the open book
there on the table beside the lit candle   but not now   now the
women lean   one toward the other   both inward   into the
distance between them   small   a very small distance that closes
as their bodies   the bodies of the two women   lovers
becomes close   so close   two women whose bodies become
close in a small room with a bright light through the window and
an open book   the book   unread   as the women move into
the distance between them   all of this they   the eyes that watch
see   watching from just outside the frame   two lovers   women
both she   the one lover   and she   the lover   the other   two
women   and the distance closing   one body close to another in
a small room at the end of two streets joining,

Sheryda Warrener

Catherine Warrener

Sheryda Warrener was born in Grimsby, Ontario. After high school she attended the University of Victoria's Creative Writing Program, from which she graduated with a BFA. She then moved to Japan, where she taught English in various cities around the Kanto area, including Tokyo. For her last year in Japan, she taught in private kindergartens. She has recently returned to Canada, currently in Victoria.

Letter Home

The moon has nothing to do with it. The moon
is a moon and has little to do with this, this *when,* this asking.

Today from the train I saw a man pissing into a carrot patch. Why do I stay?
Flowers are cheap here: gloriosa, tiger orchid, gerber daisy.
Cheap enough to buy a bunch a week, not wait
for them to die before bringing more home.

Translate moon into some unearthly language, what does it become?
An old fisherman shoring an empty boat.
The fisherman's heart as he steers the empty boat home.

SEAMS

Sliver of fish bone, vein of insect wing,
the hinge of the screen door, intricate seams.

Yesterday, the blizzard, today
everything melts and in the kitchen
you're forcing crocuses.

Your marriage has shifted.
Moths in the closet chew their way through
a bag of summer clothes.

Everything held together by the sun,
that one rusting bolt.

THIS IS A LOVE POEM

for the mouse's heart, the grapefruit seed,
the heron in the marsh beside the highway,
blue wings cut out from the sky.
For my father's laugh, the lampshade's amber
ring of light and what it illuminates:
a guitar pick, a full ashtray.
For the underside of rocks,
sting of nettle in darkness.

For the crow who flew over me
breaking the stillness of those woods
with two wingbeats like breath.

Reminding me there is noise,
and then there is quiet.

PRAISE FOR THE STARFISH

Asterias rubens,
your name mellifluous from my mouth,
though *rubens* means common
and you mean everything but.
You are fluid, slow as morning,
with your five, sometimes fifty arms.
You're the only star breathing underwater,
and I'm stunned by your patience;
being asthmatic, I've had to relearn
the essence of breath.

For twenty years I lived without
knowing your shape in my hand.
Since Gabriola, where I held you for the first time,
I've seen you everywhere: the dogwood beside my house,
it's white petals open-armed to the wind.
The asterisk stamped on every page I write,
a pause, filling white space, and you
waving your arms in your star language.

Sometimes my hands are awkward stars
clinging to solid things, people
who lead me through this world.

When the ark was full,
the last invited clambering on,
their black and white hair glistening

with those first fat drops,
you clung to rock,
green, orange, purple,
ready for the storm.

BALANCE

1.

This world
stares blankly at itself, opposes what?
Wing replies *wing,* key replies *key,* sleeve
replies *sleeve,*
cuff,
button.
Where have all the opposites gone?
        of goldfish? of wool? of poem or grief?
If anything, the trees would know,
if only our ears would tune in to their tree-noise.
For now, they clatter soundlessly to what?

2.

This world
stares blankly, opposes itself:
contentment replies *boredom,* sleep
replies *wake,*
spider replies
fox, moth replies
crow. Everything grows colder. Water replies *ice.*
A similar clambering, now heavy, clumsy, as if people
or cows could do it. So where's the magic?
In the light, the shade of: heron, iris, birch.

3.

The poem manages itself under this weight,
though it has little to do with this movement through the world. It
  holds
its own, but barely more than that: a few apples in a bowl, a fishing rod,
  a chair.
A man pinning clothes to a line, his back a kind of moon for the woman
  who watches
from their kitchen window. She hums a note or two from a song
she would never let on she knew.

HEIRLOOM

Glass apple on the windowsill. Akin to light, akin to water.
History of the chair closest to the fireplace, your mother's
mother weaved anything from wicker, her hands never tired.
That's the story someone tells you now, though you're not sure why;
they sit here with stories in their blood and nothing to tie them to.
You wait, think you see the apple spinning from the sill,
when it hits the ground it doesn't break.

Zoe Whittall

Kelly Clipperton

Zoe Whittall grew up on a sheep farm in South Durham, Quebec. She graduated from the New School in Montreal before spending two years at Concordia in the Creative Writing department. She is the author the poetry collection *The Best Ten Minutes of Your Life* (McGilligan, 2001) and the editor of the short fiction anthology *Geeks, Misfits and Outlaws* (McGilligan, 2003). She writes a column in the zine *Kiss Machine*, co-writes the comic book *Self-Serve* and reviews books and music for a variety of Canadian publications. Her work has appeared in the anthologies *Ribsauce* (Vehicule), *Brazen Femme: Queering Femininity* (Arsenal Pulp), *Girls Who Bite Back* (Sumach) and *Bent* (Women's Press). She's currently working on a collection of short stories entitled *Bottle Rocket Hearts*.

Linda Lovelace Died Today

I wake up dizzy.

Dry mouth in a full bathtub.

The washing machine catches fire and fills the house with smoke. Once the windows are open, the sparks smothered, the cat digs her nail under mine.

Swell with me.

Linda Lovelace died today.

Kate calls: "I didn't ask you to be in my porn because you have a real career now, not because you're fat."

"Huh? My washing machine is on fire. I have to go."

Lowering my arms that hold out for love into the white basin that won't drain, skin grey in blackening water. Sheets stained, soaking up hot knots of oxygen.

I call Kate back. "Linda Lovelace made *Deep Throat* at gunpoint. I overheard someone saying that on the bus and they were laughing."

I open each window,
phone cradled in my soft neck
palms against wooden ledge painted over many times,
breathing in air instead of gagging
on the smoke.

There is a man outside picking up bottles.
He is singing sweetly.
I expect him to spit but

instead he stares.

Stiff Little Fingers

Out of boredom, I was in love with the boy who sold drugs in the parkette across the street from my first apartment.

He worked at the graveyard on Mount Royal. Wore human bones around his neck. He smelled like I imagined a rock star would: gamey and gross but in a sexy way.

"You know, it's not like a final resting place. If you're family doesn't pay up, you're outta there to make room for paying customers."

He sees bodies every day. No wonder he never calls his mother, has a heroin 'situation,' that look, that smell. At my telemarketing job I think about his long fingers
cupping my shoulders, his greying lips kissing mine.

After a month, he'd topped my earthy pile of loser ex-boyfriends. He called too much. Owed me money. Probably stole my bike, the cherry one with the skull-and-crossbones stickers.

People say he's in jail, rapping his knuckles against the iron bars, scraping skin. Thinking of me, maybe, wearing his old plaid shirts as I paint my new apartment. Looking for another guy who takes himself too seriously, or just takes too much.

I love the addicts, they'll never put me first. A piece of the pie—in the grand scheme of things, I will only be a piece. Always out of reach. My own fingers, out of his.

Six Thoughts on a Parkdale Porch

1.

Last fall I had a wisdom tooth pulled by a macho dentist whose nitrous machine didn't work. Through the window I watched a woman in cut-off sweatshorts throw her red pumps at a guy in plaid pants while the dentist sewed up my three stitches.

He called me tough.

My lover kept the tooth in a small tube meant for cocaine on a string around her neck. I mistook her action for devotion when it was simply the act of accessorizing.

2.

I like the first day of a bruise waking.

A June bug is making out with the porch light again.

S m a s hing up and burning, repeat: a giant ladybug with vertigo.

The dog barks at the ceramic bunny who was made to smile constantly. Porch ornaments.

I feel defeated pinching the bruise around its edge; my thumb and fingernail are making skinny hearts.

Starving is not holy.

3.

I'm nervous. Expecting sutures instead of flat skin.

I am waiting.

My eyebrows are giving me panic attacks.
Two perfect circle blisters.

4.

Toronto Welcomes the Pope. Suddenly even the guy who punches people outside the 7-11 is a believer.

Pilgrims are selling memorabilia on my way to work at the café on Roncesvalles. Uniform-red shoulder bags walking in packs, singing hymns.

Indignant invasions around my red streetcar seat.

Two giant blue cups of water for the pregnant woman at table #2.

The cops sweep up undesirables—
*please step back and allow the holy visitors to enjoy
an unobstructed view.*

I sweep up the café floor.

At 3 a.m. on Church street, red-shouldered boys with Jesus t-shirts kiss each other on the steps outside Second Cup. Ecstasy jaws and groping in the shadows, where the Lord was not invited.

5.

I almost died in a freight elevator on my way to get laid
by someone twice my age I couldn't even really talk to.

I chewed my nails until they bled, watered down prayers
when the box went black and the cables paused.
Ridiculous faith when fingers crossed.
I wish I may, I wish I might.

The click and whir of being saved

by invention.

6.

Today, I kicked the bank machine.

The mechanics of frustration; other people's receipts stuck to my
boot.

Acknowledgements

Armstrong, Tammy: "A Proper Burial for Songbirds," "To Beat a Thunder Shower," "Reflection on What Was Missing" and "Hockey" from *Bogman's Music*, Anvil Press, 2001. Reprinted courtesy of Anvil Press.

Benning, Sheri: "Bearletter/2" and "Russian Thistle" from *Earth After Rain*, Thistledown, 2001. Reprinted courtesy of Thistledown Press.

Callanan, Mark: "The Man with the Twelve O'clock Shadow," "Divination," "Wheelbarrow" and "The Delicate Touch Required for China" from *Scarecrow*, Killick Press, 2003. Reprinted courtesy of Killick Press.

Cran, Brad: "Patterns of Leaves," "Cityscape 1," "Roseau, Dominica" and "Today After Rain" from *The Good Life*, Nightwood Editions, 2002.

Denham, Joe: "Night Haul," "Between Strings," "Gutting," "Dragging," "Morning Set" and "Bus Stop" from *Flux*, Nightwood Editions, 2003.

Dickinson, Adam: "When We Become Desirable," "Believing the First Words You Hear" and "Fort Smith Fire Brigade" from *Cartography and Walking*, Brick Books, 2002.

Finlay, Triny: "Self-Portrait As My Own Brain Tumour," "Self-Portrait As Ekphrastic Tension," "Snails," "Vinegar," "Boy" and "Pink Sneakers" from *Splitting Off*, Nightwood Editions, 2004.

Getty, Adam: "Gainful Employment," "Sonnets for Red Hill Creek" and "Steeltown" from *Reconciliation*, Nightwood Editions, 2003.

Heroux, Jason: "Fear Diary," "Story," "Dark Jars," "Evening Postscript," "Today I'm More Alive Than Usual," "The Newspaper" and "Unfurnished Apartment" from *Memoirs of an Alias*, Mansfield Press, 2004. Reprinted courtesy of Mansfield Press.

Hsu, Ray: "Benjamin: Nine Epilogues" from *Anthropy*, Nightwood Editions, 2004.

Mayor, Chandra: "Crisis House" from *August Witch*, Cyclops Press, 2002.

McOrmond, Steve: "The Burn Barrel," "Apprehension," and "Loyalist Burial Ground iv" appeared in *Lean Days*, Wolsak & Wynn, 2004. Reprinted courtesy of Wolsak & Wynn.

Murray, George: "Emblem" and "Window" from *The Hunter*, McClelland & Stewart, 2003. "The Bats" from *The Cottage Builder's Letter*, McClelland & Stewart, 2001. Reprinted courtesy of McClelland & Stewart. "The Carnie's Obituary" from *Carousel: A Book of Second Thoughts*, Exile, 2000.

Pick, Alison: "Winter: Leaving the Farm," and "'Is it raining where you are? Are you watching? Is the rain the story now?' –Helen Humphreys" from *Question & Answer*, Polestar Press, 2003. Reprinted courtesy of Polestar, an imprint of Raincoast Books.

Rhodes, Shane: "Day and Night the Sea Whispered Thalassa" from *Holding Pattern*, NeWest Press, 2000, and "Haynes Town Store" from *The Wireless Room*, NeWest Press, 2002. Reprinted courtesy of NeWest Press.

robinson, matt: "f(x)—5th metacarpal; on seeing the x-ray of your broken hand," "pitch (love poem for the montreal expos)," "notes toward an apartment story" and "a home economics" from *how we play at it: a list*, ECW Press, 2002. Reprinted courtesy of ECW Press.

Rosnau, Laisha: "Point of Exit," "On the Ground," "Central Standard" and "The Girls Are Sleeping" from *Notes on Leaving*, Nightwood Editions, 2004.

Sinclair, Sue: "Departure," "Lyric Strain" and "Saskatchewan" from *Secrets of Weather & Hope*, Brick Books, 2001. "Canoeing the St. John River" from *Mortal Arguments*, Brick Books, 2003.

Stephens, Nathalie: "Plate No. 9" and "Plate No. 14" from *Somewhere Running*, Arsenal Pulp Press, 2000. Reprinted courtesy of Arsenal Pulp Press. "Début" from *Paper City*, Coach House Books, 2003. Reprinted courtesy of Coach House Books.

Whittall, Zoe: "Stiff Little Fingers" from *The Best 10 Minutes of Your Life*, McGilligan Books, 2001. Reprinted courtesy of McGilligan Books.

Many of the poems in this book were first published in integral literary magazines such as *Grain, Arc, subTerrain, Prairie Fire, The Fiddlehead, Exile, The Malahat Review, Event, PRISM International, Contemporary Verse 2, This Magazine, Geist, The Antigonish Review, Capilano Review, Queen's Street Quarterly, Prairie Journal, Echolocation, TickleAce, Canadian Literature, filling Station* and *The Wascana Review*.